W9-ALU-705

101

Secrets A Good Dad Knows

Walter Browder and Sue Ellin Browder
Illustrations by Walter Browder

RUTLEDGE HILL PRESS®

Nashville, Tennessee

A Division of Thomas Nelson, Inc.
www.ThomasNelson.com

Copyright © 2000 by Walter Browder and Sue Ellin Browder

All rights reserved. Written permission must be secured from the publisher to use or reproduce any part of this book, except for brief quotations in critical reviews or articles.

The material in this book is meant to be used under the supervision of a responsible adult. The authors and the publisher assume no responsibility for misuse of this information.

Published by Rutledge Hill Press, Inc., a Division of Thomas Nelson, Inc., P.O. Box 141000, Nashville, Tennessee 37214.

Typography by Roger A. DeLiso, Rutledge Hill Press
Text design by Harriette Bateman

Library of Congress Cataloging-in-Publication Data
Browder, Walter, 1939–
     101 secrets a good dad knows / Walter Browder and Sue Ellin Browder; illustrations by Walter Browder.
        p.   cm.
     ISBN 1-4016-0008-5
     1. Father and child—Miscellanea.   2. Fathers—Miscellanea.   3. Curiosities and wonders.   I. Title.   II. Title: One hundred and one secrets a good dad knows. III. Browder, Sue Ellin, 1946–
HQ756.B78   1999
306.874'221—dc21   99-044983

Printed in the United States of America
 2 3 4 5 6 7 8 9—06 05 04

In loving memory of our fathers,
"Rosie" Browder and Floyd Hurdle,
who taught us that anything worth doing
is worth doing well

Contents

Thanks!

Good dads always thank people who help and support them. So a great big thanks and a round of heartfelt applause go out to:

First of all, our children, Dustin and Erin, who were always eager to learn dad skills.

Then to John Miller, Ginny Miller, John Sencak, Mike Hanrahan, Melissa Klarr, Darlene Duffield, and the many supportive people at St. John's. Also Jen Browder, Paul Wilhelm Karl Rothemund, Liz O'Neil, Alex Vera, Mike Pickering, Debra Sherman, and Jose Ramirez, who gave us wonderful insights and support.

And last, but far from least, Larry Stone, Bill Jayne, Julie Jayne, Bryan Curtis, Eugenia Harris, Jennifer Brett Greenstein, Stacie Kutzbach, and all the other great players on the Rutledge Hill team.

Remember, kids, always say please and thank-you.

Introduction

Who first taught you how to saw a board? To fly a kite? To catch a fish? Or to whistle through your teeth? If anyone taught you these sometimes whimsical, but always practical, crafts of childhood, chances are it was your dad. As you learned these simple skills, you very likely also learned: "Nothing's more rewarding than a job well done." "If at first you don't succeed, try again." Or "Never be afraid to speak out clearly for your beliefs." You picked up nuggets of knowledge that molded your character for life.

Dads have special ways of teaching kids that differ from—but are, nonetheless, just as important as—the ways mothers teach. For example, dads tend to roughhouse and tease kids more than moms do, and by doing so, they "stretch" their children's social abilities. Fathers also have highly complex and important skills to teach—"dad skills," if you will—that raise a child's self-esteem, increase self-confidence, and foster self-reliance.

So what exactly is a dad skill? Basically, it's a practical little skill or bit of knowledge that expands a child's ability to cope with or understand the world and initially requires an adult coach. Take feeding a horse, for example. If a child doesn't understand how to behave around a horse, it can be dangerous to feed one. But with a wise, patient parent (you) at his side, a child can soon enjoy the unforgettable pleasure of a horse nuzzling his hand. Sawing a board smoothly is also beyond most children's capabilities. But with your help, your daughter can soon build a bird feeder the warblers and goldfinches will love. Many dad skills—such as learning how to tell time by the North Star—also help a child more thoroughly understand his place in the universe.

Yet dad skills, by their very nature, also have far deeper value: they instill in children virtuous habits that are the essentials of good character. Learning to feed a big, powerful horse teaches a child that courage is not inborn or simply a matter of being fearless. Courage comes from knowing how to act in a scary situation and can therefore be learned. Sawing a board teaches a child the importance of both skill and patience in doing a job well. Maybe because the skills themselves are of such immediate value, the child tends to overlook the moral lesson. Yet each time the skill is used, the moral lesson is reinforced and becomes part of that great mysterious process we call character building.

The wisdom fathers possess has almost always been passed down through the generations by word-of-mouth. In fact, to our knowledge, most of the playful, practical lessons fathers have traditionally taught their kids have never been written down in one place—until now. Why bother to record in print what has essentially always been part of our culture's oral tradition? Because the skills and wisdom dads once taught their sons (and to a lesser extent, their daughters) are slowly but surely being lost. "Shinny," as in "Hey, let's shinny up a tree!" is not even in most unabridged dictionaries. Millions of boys and girls today are growing up without fathers. Many new dads who want to be more involved with their kids also grew up either without dads or with fathers who, for one reason or another, didn't take the time to pass on this knowledge. We wrote down these lessons not as lists of instructions on how to be a good father, but to ensure that there will always be good dads (and now also good moms) who will never forget "the really important stuff" hidden in such simple skills as how to climb a ladder, how to carve a whistle, and how to make a curve ball curve.

Does this mean the "101 secrets a good dad knows" are lessons only a father can teach? Not at all. A mother can easily teach her daughter or son how to use a compass, row a boat, or bait a fishhook. The problem is that many moms were never introduced to dad skills as little girls—just as many dads never learned how to prepare baby formula or change diapers. Happily, this book should help correct this inequity.

The legacy of love continues. Pass it on.

1. How to Catch a Frog

Approaching an old problem from a new angle is the essence of creative imagination. It's also the best way to catch a frog.

—A Good Dad Saying

Catching a frog is a little like netting a fairy or trapping a leprechaun. Long before they've actually seen one in a pond, kids have read stories about frogs and seen frogs as favorite characters on TV. On a summer night in the country, with their big voices, frogs seem to be everywhere. But let a kid try to catch one and the frog vanishes with a little splash—unless you know the secret that will allow your child to hold a frog, with all its awe and wonder, in his hands.

The secret is this: never approach a frog from the *bank* side of the stream or pond. The frog (who, of course, jumps away from anyone he hears coming) will instantly leap into the water. To outfox a frog, you need to approach him from the *water* side. This means (1) the water has to be fairly shallow, and (2) you and your kid have to get your feet wet.

So go barefoot or wear old shoes. Take a large plastic bowl with you and quietly wade well out in the water before turning toward the croaking frog.

Even if the frog does hear you coming, chances are he'll hop *away* from the water. Once he's on land, you can move much faster than he can, so go after him. When the time is right, pop the bowl over him.

You can also catch a frog at night by using a flashlight. Sneak up on the frog from the water side. Suddenly flick on the flashlight and blind him with the bright light.

Once he's caught, of course, the frog (being an amphibian) needs water to live in. And when it's time to release him back to the wild, be sure to let him go near water—unless, of course, you like frog legs.

DAD FACT

Is It a Frog or a Toad?

Frogs have smooth, moist, shiny skin, whereas a toad's skin is rough, dry, and somewhat lumpy. (The lumps are often erroneously called "warts," but contrary to popular myth, touching a toad won't give you warts.) Frogs always live near water, while toads can live in much drier places—even in the desert. A toad, having shorter hind legs and a wider, clumsier body than a frog, also moves a lot slower and is much easier to catch. That's why when you've caught a speedy frog, you've pulled off a real coup.

2. How to Identify Six Big Airplanes

In 1910, "competent experts" predicted the airplane had no commercial future because it would never be able to carry more than five or six people. Moral: the naysayers are often wrong. Always keep a dream in your pocket.

—A Good Dad Reflection

Kids are fascinated with intercontinental airplanes. But they hardly ever see one up close unless they're taking a trip. As you stand in the terminal of a sprawling international airport, it may seem to your kid as if all big planes are the same.

Yet you know how to tell large planes apart as easily as you can tell a hawk from a crow. The secret: like birds, big planes fit into certain categories that allow you to tell them apart. First check their wings. Then look at their tails. Here's how to identify six of the most common:

Four engines (two under each wing): It's either a Boeing 747 or a new plane in the Airbus A300 series. If it has a hump on its back, it's a 747 (figure a); if it doesn't, it's an Airbus (figure b). This new Airbus is also the only plane that has two rows of passenger windows running the full length of the plane.

Three engines (one under each wing and one on the tail): If it has no visible exhaust on its tail, it's an L-1011 (figure c). If it has a visible exhaust, it's either a Boeing MD-11 or a DC-10. If its wing tips turn up, it's an MD-11 (figure d). If they don't, it's a DC-10 (figure e).

No engines under the wings, three around the tail: It's a Boeing 727 (figure f). This plane also has no visible exhaust.

As your child learns the names of these big planes, she can also learn that the feats of today's technology began as a dream. Through work, dedication, and insight, the "impossible" was accomplished. So if anyone warns your child not to let her dreams get too big, she can tell them she already knows the names of six big dreams that are now commonplace on air routes around the world.

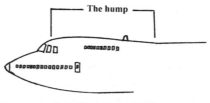

(a) Boeing 747

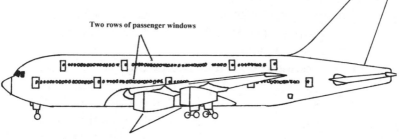

(b) Airbus

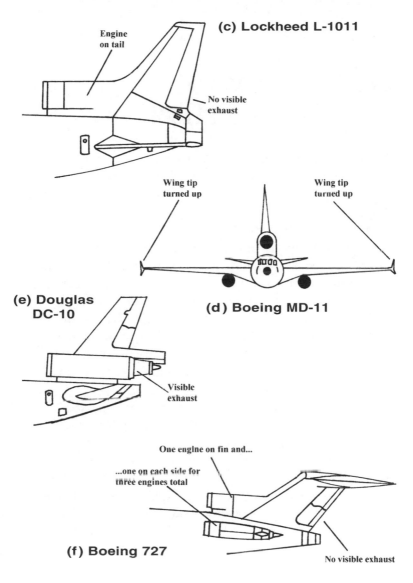

(c) Lockheed L-1011

Engine on tail

No visible exhaust

Wing tip turned up

Wing tip turned up

(e) Douglas DC-10

(d) Boeing MD-11

Visible exhaust

One engine on fin and...

...one on each side for three engines total

(f) Boeing 727

No visible exhaust

17

3. How to Put a Worm on a Hook

You wouldn't eat a sandwich that's been wadded up and crammed in a sack. So why treat a worm, a fish's lunch, that way?

—A Good Dad Observation

When a child first goes bait fishing, he'll try to thread a worm on the hook sort of like he'd put a sock on his foot—and possibly impale his thumb in the process. Or he'll wad up the worm, running the hook through it so many times that any self-respecting fish would turn away in disgust.

As the dad adage goes, "to catch a fish, you have to think like a fish." This means that to the fish, the bait has to look delicious. So show your child how to hook a worm in a way that's most appetizing to a fish: through the enlarged band, also known as the sex collar.

First, have your kid notice that worms are segmented (that is, they have little lines all around their bodies). Now have him observe that one segment of the worm is relatively long and smooth. That's the enlarged band, the best place for him to attach the hook.

Have him insert the hook at one end of the enlarged band, pass the point through the worm's body, and then bring the point back up through the other end of the enlarged band (see illustration). He wants to hide as much of the hook as possible from the fish.

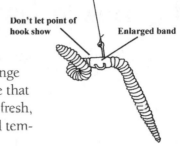

Don't let point of hook show

Enlarged band

If the fish hasn't bitten after about thirty minutes, your kid might want to exchange the worm on the hook for one that looks fresher. To keep worms fresh, he should store them at a cool temperature of 40 to 60 degrees Fahrenheit. He should also make sure they get plenty of air. (Oxygen keeps worms looking tasty.)

By showing your child this technique, you're helping him catch more fish. At the same time, you're teaching him the importance of neat work—shoddy work always shows. Even a fish knows sloppy work when he sees it, and even a fish doesn't like it.

DAD TIP

Next time you take your kid trout fishing, try using Power Bait instead of your usual worm. Power Bait has the consistency of putty and comes in little jars of iridescent yellow, green, or pink. It's very easy to use. Your kid simply takes a small wad and squeezes it onto the hook. Nobody knows exactly why Power Bait works so well. But for trout fishing, it can't be beat.

4. How to Saw a Board

There's something very honest about a cleanly sawed board.

—A Good Dad Saying

There are two noticeable types of people in the world: those who build and those who tear down what others have built. Start your child on the road to being a builder; teach her how to use a saw.

Used incorrectly, a sharp-toothed steel saw will leave a board scarred and unevenly cut. Worse, a child can injure herself. But used correctly, a saw can build a birdhouse the robins or goldfinches will love. The secret: take off just a little wood at a time.

Here's a four-step procedure for making smooth, honest cuts.

1. Get into the position to cut. Your child should place her knee on the board to steady it. If she's sawing with her right hand, she should put her left knee on the board. If she's left-handed, she should use her right knee.

2. Her first inclination may be to jam the saw down hard to start the kerf (the saw cut). But this can cause the teeth to bite deep, making an ugly cut. So, instead, she should draw the saw back slowly across the wood. This knocks off the board's initial sharp corner and makes a slight groove in the wood.

3. Have her make long, smooth strokes. Each time she pushes forward, the saw cuts the wood. Each time she pulls back, the saw pulls dust out of the cut. If her strokes are too short, she won't get all the sawdust out. Eventually, the saw will ride on top of the loose dust, cut poorly, and finally lock up. How long should her strokes be? About three inches shorter than the length of the saw's cutting edge.

4. As she approaches the end of the cut, have your child saw more slowly and lightly. She should use her free hand to support the piece of wood that's about to fall off. If she doesn't, the little, unsawed piece will break off, leaving an unsightly spike.

With what you've taught her, she'll have a perfectly smooth cut from beginning to end. And each time she uses a saw, she'll remember it's not just force that gets the job done; it's muscle skillfully applied with patience and care. Good, honest labor builds character as well as projects. You want the best in both.

5. How to Get the Honey Out of a Honeysuckle

Life's sweetest fruits aren't always forbidden.

—Good Dad Observation

Kids love treasure hunts for goodies. They especially enjoy Easter egg hunts in which countless sweets are secreted away under bushes and behind flowers. The only trouble is that a kid has to wait for an adult like you to buy the candy and hide it.

Wouldn't a kid love it if, just once, Mother Nature would provide a treasure hunt he could enjoy without waiting for you?

Well, it just so happens, she has. She has hidden sweet nectar in a honeysuckle.

So the next time you're in that fragrant meadow your kid loves to hike or in grandmother's blossom-scented garden, show your child how to find one of life's "secret" sweets: show him how to get the honey out of a honeysuckle.

The best honeysuckle for this adventure is the dwarf bush variety, which produces small, yellow blossoms. But any honeysuckle will work.

To sample the nectar, simply have your child grip the top of the funnel-shaped floret between his thumb and forefinger and pull the flower loose from the green cup in which it sits. Then with his fingernail have him pinch off the bottom of the blossom, the end that used to rest in the cup. By sucking on this end, he can get the honey. Or he can squeeze the flower tip between his thumb and forefinger, forcing the elixir out in little golden drops. Mmmmm! Sweet! It's enough to make a hummingbird hum.

After he's sampled a few flowers, encourage your child to share this secret with a friend. As the summer progresses and more flowers pop out, he and his friends can have as many treasure hunts as they please.

And while he's hunting out the flowers, he'll also be learning that life sometimes contains sweet secrets we all too often overlook. We just have to know where to find them.

**Pluck out floret,
pinch off end**

6. How to Identify a Poisonous Snake

Knowledge is power, mostly over fear.

—A Good Dad Saying

Snakes can run without legs and climb without arms. Wet-looking, even in the desert, these slippery creatures almost seem to be alien life forms, able to kill with a single bite. So when kids see a snake in the woods, they either want to get away from it fast or kill it. Both are empty-headed responses to fear.

With a little insight, your kid can do better. Teach him how to tell, immediately, if a snake is poisonous. Simply have him look at its head. Nonpoisonous reptiles, such as the plains garter snake (figure a), have long, narrow heads. But a whopping 99 percent of poisonous snakes in North America have wide, triangle-shaped heads. That's because they're pit vipers—snakes that have long hollow fangs and use "pits" on the sides of their heads to sense the little warm-blooded animals they like to eat. Rattlesnakes (figure b), cottonmouths (also called water moccasins), and copperheads are all pit vipers.

So the next time your kid and his friends encounter a stray

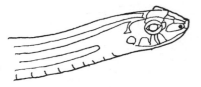

(a) Plains garter snake

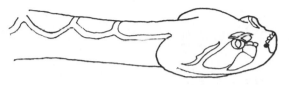

snake on the trail, while the others are panicking, he'll be studying the creature.

(b) Western diamondback rattlesnake   Remembering that snakes can strike only about half their own length (another fact you've passed on), he'll also know he and his friends are perfectly safe so long as they leave the reptile alone.

By showing your child how to look for the wide, triangular head, you've instilled in him the right attitude toward snakes—watchful, but unfrightened. Also, you've taught him something else. With the right knowledge, he can judge danger for himself. And that's the first step in learning independence.

DAD FACT

Do All Poisonous Snakes Have Wide Heads?

No. India's deadly kraits and Africa's black mambas have narrow heads. So do many other snakes around the world. But in North America, there's only one narrow-headed poisonous snake: the coral snake. Rarely seen because it usually hunts underground, the coral snake is ringed in red, yellow, and black, with red outlining yellow. The similar, but harmless, king snake has red, yellow, and black, with red rings outlined by black. Your child can easily remember the difference with this simple rhyme: "Red on black, friend of Jack. Red on yellow, kill a fellow."

7. How to Row a Boat

Everyone must row with the oars he has.

—A Good Dad Proverb

The child who can row a boat has mastered a lesson in self-reliance she can use all her life. But for a child, boating can be dangerous unless she learns how to do it correctly from a knowledgeable adult like you. So after stressing the importance of always wearing a life jacket and other safety tips, here's how to get her started.

Basically, the secret of rowing is understanding that the oars are levers. When rowing, she has to apply energy to those levers to move the boat through the water.

1. Show her the oarlocks, those U-shaped, pivoting supports on the gunwales (upper edges of the boat's sides) in which the oars rest. These are the fulcrums of the levers. Place the oars in the oarlocks so when the handles are positioned in front of your child's chest, they just touch or slightly overlap each other. This gives her maximum leverage.

2. Now, she should brace herself to apply lots of force. Remember, she's moving the whole boat and passengers. She should place her feet against the ribs in the bottom of the boat for support and lean forward. Have her extend her hands, holding the oars in front of her, with arms out straight. Now have her raise the oar handles so the blades dip about halfway underwater.

3. She should begin to pull by straightening up and using her leg and back muscles to bring the oar handles in close to her chest. She may want to lean over backwards a bit. That's okay. As she pulls, the boat will glide backward for her.

4. Once she completes her pull, have her lower her hands and lift the oars out of the water.

5. Finally, she should straighten her arms and lean forward. Then as she lifts her hands and dips the oars back in the water, she's ready for another stroke.

Once she's mastered the technique of levering the boat through the water, encourage her to row for a while. Although she'll be rowing backwards, don't direct her. Eventually, as confidence in her abilities grows, she'll learn to row straight. It's sort of a case of learning how to get ahead without always knowing where you're going.

8. How to Carve a Whistle

The difference between a useless stick and a useful stick is in the person who picks it up.

—A Good Dad Saying

It takes no special virtue to buy a whistle. But whittling one from a tree branch requires patience, persistence, and effort. Besides, a store-bought whistle has a store-bought sound. A carved whistle makes a sound so unique it's as if you'd sung all those little "wheets" yourself.

So how, your kid wonders, can you hollow out a stick without cutting it apart or boring a hole? The secret: tree branches have a neat little covering he can take off and replace. It's called bark. With the clever use of bark, he can craft a whistle in a matter of minutes.

First, have your kid cut a green stick about ½ inch thick and 5 or 6 inches long. He'll want a fresh branch with no knots or twigs and a smooth bark. Ash and willow are good, but many other woods will also work.

1. He should cut off end A of this stick squarely. Then about 2½ inches from end A (at C), he should use a sharp knife to cut the whole way around the stick. He should cut only bark deep (figure a).

2. Next have him cut a small, V-shaped notch in the stick (at B), about 1½ inches from the squared-off end. He should always carve away from—not towards—himself.

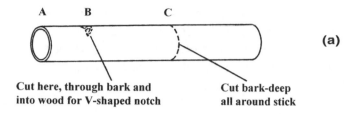

A   B   C

(a)

Cut here, through bark and into wood for V-shaped notch

Cut bark-deep all around stick

3. Have him wet the whistle from end A to cut C by dipping it in water. Then, resting the stick on his thigh, have him use his knife handle to tap gently on the bark from A to C. As he taps, he should keep turning the stick and wetting it regularly. He's working to bruise the bark so it will lift easily away from the stick. He should test occasionally by grabbing the bark firmly and twisting. When it's free, the bark will rotate on the stick.

4. Now, he should carefully slide the bark from end A, keeping the bark cylinder intact.

5. To create the cavity (figure b), have him make two straight cuts about halfway into the stick until he gets to

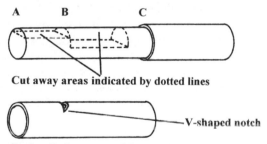

A   B   C

Cut away areas indicated by dotted lines

V-shaped notch

Bark cylinder removed from end A

(b)

the pith (core)—the first cut at the V-notch B, the second about 1½ inches farther along the stick. Then have him whittle away the wood between these two cuts (as shown).

6. Now he should slice a thin sliver of wood off the top of the stick from A to B. Removing this wood provides a channel for air passage, so when he blows into the whistle at A, the air will reach the carved-out cavity. If there's no air passage, there's no sound.

7. Finally, he should slide the bark cylinder carefully back on the stick, blow lightly, and . . . *tweet*!

In an age of machines, your kid has just gained a new respect for human ingenuity: it can even coax a high-tech sound out of an old stick. Innovation never ends.

DAD SAFETY TIP

Though sharp whittling knives look dangerous, they're actually safer than a knife that's too dull. But do make sure your child is old enough to handle knives before teaching this skill. Once your child is old enough to carve a whistle, he should always carve away from—not towards—himself. It's also a good idea to get a whittling glove from a craft store. It will protect his non-whittling hand from cuts.

9. How to Catch a Baseball

Willie Mays is sixth on the all-time list for games played, tenth for slugging average, eighth for at bats, ninth for hits, third for home runs, fifth for runs scored, and seventh for runs batted in. Yet he's most remembered for "the catch" in the 1954 World Series.

—A Good Dad Observation

When catching a baseball, a beginner usually thinks the glove does it all. So he holds out the glove, keeps his hand firm, and waits for the ball to be "trapped" in the vast recesses of webbing and pocket. Keeping his hand tight and stiff, he develops "hard hands." And, as a good dad knows, hard hands don't catch many baseballs.

The secret to helping your child develop "soft" hands, which *do* catch balls, is to have him practice catching barehanded. If a baseball's too hard for him to catch bare-handed at first, he can begin with a light plastic ball.

Teach him how to hold his hands: palms facing out with (1) fingers down to catch balls below his waist or (2) fingers up for balls above his waist. Then show him how to close on the ball, with his fingers relaxed, not stiff and tense.

Now show him how to "give" with his hands, letting them travel slightly away from the ball as it arrives. Catching the ball with "give" absorbs some of its energy and lessens its impact, so it won't sting.

Once he's got this down pat, let him put on that glove. But remind him to keep allowing his hands to give a little—not too much, but just enough to make his hands "soft." Eventually, he'll learn to do this without even thinking about it.

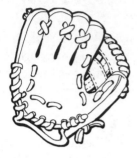

There are, of course, more skills to catching than having soft hands—fielding a fly ball up near his head, so he can throw it quickly, for example. But he'll learn these other skills, too, as he goes along. And while he's developing the patience and determination to catch a ball well, he'll also be learning another lesson: it's important to have good technology, whether it's a faster computer or a baseball glove that helps us catch better. But he should never forget, it's the human hand behind that technology that really makes things work.

10. How to Use a Hoe

A man of words and not of deeds is like a garden full of weeds.
　　　　　　　　　　　　　　　　　　—A Good Dad Saying

Kids take one look at a hoe and think, "Chop, chop, chop!" They chop the weeds. They chop the earth. And sometimes, losing control, they chop the vegetables or flowers. But you know hoeing is one of those slow, gentle, patient things we do for the earth. Tilling the soil is an act of friendship.

So first have your child look at the hoe. Point out its thin blade and long, spindly handle—neither is designed for heavy chopping. Have her notice the hoe is bent like a plow. This means as she pulls it, it will tend to dig into the ground like a plow, with little effort. (A hoe that doesn't dig easily into the earth usually simply needs to be sharpened.)

Second, show your child how to hold the hoe, with her hands well apart on the handle (not together, the way she'd hold a baseball bat or an ax). Have her place one hand on the hoe near her hip. This is her "pulling hand." Have her place the other hand about a foot to eighteen inches down the handle. This is her "weight hand"— the one she'll use to press down on the hoe as she pulls it back.

Now teach her to hoe with little short strokes. She needs to dig gently under the weeds to uproot them, not chop them off. At the same time, she's loosening the dirt, turning it over to get fresh nitrogen to the roots of the vegetables or flowers.

Mastering this simple skill will give your child an irreplaceable avocation. As she learns to care for the plants, she'll also learn the sacred relationship of sky, sun, and earth. And someday, alone in her garden with the sun warm on her back, she will thank you for it.

11. How to Tie a Fly

Catching a fish is just the excuse we use to get to tie flies.
—A Good Dad Reflection

Once long ago in the green of the world, a man observed that fish eat lots of bugs. Then he discovered he could tie objects like feathers or deer hair on a fish hook to make it look like a bug. When he dropped his disguised hook in the water, it was so light it didn't sink. That's when fishing stopped being a sport and became an art. Ever since, dads have taught their kids to tie flies. But this is a complicated craft. So introduce your kid to it by showing her how to tie a fly that's simple, but looks good enough to eat on ice cream—fish ice cream, that is.

The secret to catching a fish with a tied fly is to be able to mimic many insects. The fly has to "match the hatch," as they say. Your child can try this one. Let her start with a tail. Then she can go on to make the body, the wings, and the head.

Before she starts, she should get a small vice or locking pliers to hold the hook steady while she works. Then she should get thread, a short piece of yarn (yellow or brown), small feathers like those from a rooster's nape, a small hook, a pair of scissors, and waterproof glue.

1. Have her begin by tying the thread onto the shank (straight part of the hook), just under the eye (hole where the hook ties onto the fishing line). She should tie it securely and cut off the loose end (figure a).

2. Have her add a few feathers for a tail and secure them to the hook by wrapping them with the thread to the shank (figure b). Knot the thread.

3. Now show her how to attach the piece of yarn and secure it with another knot in the thread (figure c). She should wrap both thread and yarn on the shank all the way back to the eye (figure d). Then knot the thread and cut off the loose end of the yarn. She shouldn't knot the yarn because that would be too bulky. She also shouldn't cut off the thread.

4. Now on top of the "bug," she'll attach some feathers for wings and securely wrap those with the thread. Finally, have her wrap the thread around the shank several times to simulate a head. Knot it twice and cut off the thread. Then have her add just a dab of glue to secure the knots (figure e). She now has a fly some fish will love.

Still, it's a lesson in humility to try tying a fly a fish might like. If the fish spurns the fly she's made, your kid can't catch him. There's something very humbling about waiting for a fish to pass judgment on your work.

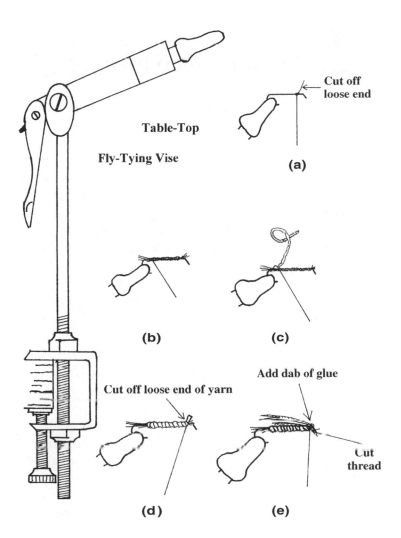

Table-Top

Fly-Tying Vise

Cut off loose end

(a)

(b)

(c)

Cut off loose end of yarn

(d)

Add dab of glue

Cut thread

(e)

37

12. How to Feed a Horse

Good fun always passes by
He who is afraid to try.

—A Good Dad Saying

To a child, horses are lots of fun, but they also have hammers for feet and a nutcracker for a mouth—and they're very, very scary. What a child does not know is that most horses are gentle giants who would never hurt anyone on purpose. (For the few ornery ones who might bite or kick, check "How a Horse 'Talks'" below).

To make sure the horse is friendly, you may first want to feed it yourself. Hold your hand out with the fingers completely extended, your palm and fingers making a flat platform. Lay some granulated sugar or a bit of apple in the middle of this platform. Offer the tidbit with the heel of your hand above the horse's upper lip and the tips of your fingers well below his lower lip. Never let your fingers curl around the offered tidbit. The horse can open its mouth unbelievably wide and could nibble your fingers by mistake. As the horse nuzzles your hand and crunches the tidbit, explain to your child what you're doing.

Once you know the horse is safe, your child will undoubtedly be eager to feed it. Just one note: if his hand is so small that the horse might accidentally get his jaws around it, skip the apple and go with the granulated sugar instead. A horse will pick up an apple or a sugar cube with his teeth, but he'll pick up granulated sugar with his *tongue*.

Feeding a horse is often a slobbery business. But as your child stands there giggling with delight, he will have learned that true courage isn't simply a matter of being fearless, but of knowing how to handle himself in a scary situation.

DAD FACT

How a Horse "Talks"

A happy, friendly horse has relaxed lips and kind, calm eyes. His ears are pricked up or relaxed sideways. But a horse thinking about biting holds his lips tensely open, with his teeth exposed, his ears flat against his head, and a nasty glint in his eye. His tail may also be clamped down hard or swishing violently. Sometimes a young horse (under age three) will "snap" or "jaw wave." This looks as if he's about to bite, but he's actually saying, "I'm young and harmless. Please don't hurt me." In case of doubt, always ask an experienced horseman to translate the animal's moods or intentions.

13. How to Fly a Kite

God, give me the serenity to accept the things I cannot change, the courage to change the things I can, and the wisdom to know the difference.

—The Serenity Prayer

Nothing can be more fun for a kid on a spring day than watching her kite climb toward the clouds. And nothing can be more depressing than returning home with a dirty, broken victim of the capricious wind. But a smashed kite needn't happen. Once your child learns the secret to flying a single-line kite (a single-line Delta is a good first kite to buy), she'll never again allow a fair April breeze to bully her.

The secret is this: when she pulls on the line, she bends the spar (that little stick running across the back of the kite). This gives the kite shape and makes it want to fly in the direction it's aimed. When the spar is bent, the kite will go up if it's aimed up and down if it's aimed down.

Letting the string go slack has just the opposite effect; her kite will flatten out, lose its shape, and no longer want to go in any direction. So it tries to go in every direction and spins.

Give your child the following information: the second the top of her kite points in the direction she wants it to travel—like *up*—she should pull the string tight, bending the spar and giving the kite shape. It will soar toward the clouds. The second her kite points in a direction she doesn't want it to travel—like *down*—she should let up on the line until the kite starts spinning.

When she gets that sinking feeling in the pit of her stomach because her kite has turned over and begun a long plunge toward the ground, it takes a lot of gumption to resist yanking that string. But that's what she must do. She must resist the urge to seize control. She has to loosen the string and let the kite spin until it points up. Only then should she take charge and tighten the line. Her kite will once again sail towards the clouds.

With this secret and a little practice, your child will be able to make her kite do figure eights and dive within inches of the ground before climbing again, like a stunt flyer in an aerial circus. She'll also learn it's important to invest her energy in those things she can change and let go of things beyond her control.

DAD TIP

Controlling How Fast a Kite Changes Direction

To make a kite spin faster, attach a wad of chewing gum (or putty) to the lower part of the center spine. Try one-fourth to one-half ounce (that's four to eight pieces of freshly chewed Juicy Fruit) to see how it works. To get a faster spin, add more.

To make a kite spin slower, add a tail. Start with a 1½-inch strip of crepe paper, 2 or 3 feet long. With this much tail, the kite will spin very slowly. Adjust the spin by cutting off more and more tail until the kite changes directions at the speed you want.

---

14. How to Find the North Star

Like Polaris, be steady in your habits, so others may rely on you.
—A Good Dad Adage

Nearly all stars change their locations, depending on the time of day and the season. Even the sun and the moon move. To a child in this ever-changing world, it may seem there's no stability in the heavens. But one star is constant: the North Star (Polaris). Once your child has spotted it, he can count on finding it in the same place again and again.

For all its fame, the North Star is surprisingly dim. Trying to pick it out right away in the middle of all those other stars is a bit like looking for a snowflake in a snowdrift. The secret to finding Polaris is this: first, find the Big Dipper. It's one of the most distinctive constellations in the sky.

Take your child out on a clear night to a meadow, broad lawn, rooftop—anyplace with an unobstructed view. Then face north, and have him look for the Big Dipper. It rotates around Polaris, so sometimes it's high in the sky and other times just above the horizon. Once you've found it, point out the two stars at the end of the Big Dipper's cup. One is named Merak. The other is Dubhe. These are the "pointer stars." They point to Polaris. Have your child imagine a straight line drawn from Merak through Dubhe

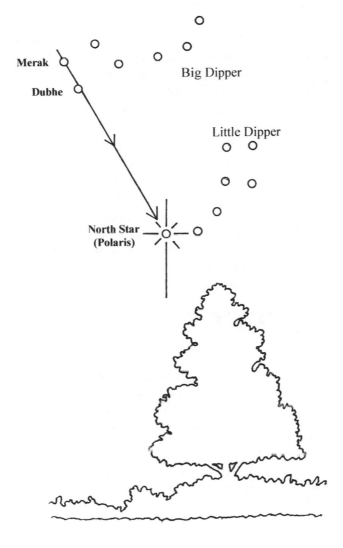

Merak

Dubhe

Big Dipper

Little Dipper

North Star
(Polaris)

and on beyond—until it touches Polaris (see figure). Polaris is the last star in the handle of the Little Dipper.

Tell him to memorize the star's location (for example, right above the sycamore in your neighbor's yard). Explain it will always be there. Spring, summer, fall, or winter. Early at night or very late. Even if he returns to this spot when he has grandchildren of his own, Polaris will still be there—exactly where he found it for the first time. The Big Dipper, the Little Dipper, and all the other stars rotate, but Polaris stays steadfast.

Explain that Polaris is an old friend of travelers because after dark, it's the easiest way to find north. Dads have not always taught their kids about math, kites, or the compass because those were only invented in the past few thousand years. But, surely, since man first began building civilizations, he's taught his kids about the North Star.

DAD FACT

Polaris

If your child were to point a camera at Polaris and leave the lens open for several hours, he would see circular trails made by the other stars as the Earth turns. But because it never moves, Polaris would appear as a bright, stable dot. If your child stood at the North Pole, Polaris would be directly overhead. If he stood at the equator, it would be on the horizon. In the continental United States—about halfway between the equator and the North Pole—Polaris is about halfway up the sky.

15. How to Whistle through Your Fingers

The man who can sing opera makes us all glad, but the man who can whistle through his fingers gets the cab.

—A Good Dad Saying

Kids are little people with little voices. All too often, they get overlooked and ignored. Yet, at times, a child needs to make a big noise. And one of the biggest of all noises is the ear-splitting, taxi-stopping, through-your-fingers whistle. When a child does it, she'll get everybody's attention. No one will believe a noise that big came out of somebody so small.

Like most confidence-boosting skills, whistling through your fingers takes effort to learn. You can't simply hand your kid this ability on a silver platter. But you can coach her. And while you're at it, you might also want to encourage a certain amount of restraint. No one should be subjected to this shrill sound in, say, an elevator.

To learn to whistle through her fingers:

1. Have your child draw her lower lip firmly across and slightly below the tops of her lower teeth.

2. Now have her put the tips of her pinkie fingers together at about a forty-five-degree angle. Have her place the tips of her pinkies against the tip of her tongue, pushing her tongue up and slightly back. Her tongue will be wadded up, sort of like an accordion. Her pinkies will rest on her lower teeth, just short of the first joint.

3. When her fingers are positioned correctly, you'll be able to see a little triangular hole formed by her pinkie fingers and lower teeth.

4. Have her close her lips firmly around her fingers so no air can escape (very important). Now have her blow forcefully through the little triangular hole.

At first, she probably won't get a whistle—just the soft, whooshing sound of blowing air. But this is normal. Encourage her to keep trying. Have her experiment by bringing her fingers closer together, pinching the air off, then blowing faster or slower. Have her keep varying her whistle until she gets a tweet.

She'll probably need to practice lots over the next several weeks. But tell her not to give up. Eventually, with diligent effort, she'll hear the faintest catch of a whistle, or maybe a brief full-blown blast. And when she does, she's almost there. Soon she'll be signaling to the peanut vendor at the ball game when he's so far away it'd take a strong-armed right fielder to hurl the peanut bag to her seat.

Little people can make big noises and sometimes should. It just requires a little dad knowledge anybody can teach. With the fortitude to keep practicing, she may not get bigger, but she'll sound like she did. And if she's got a sound that big in her, she's going to think twice about what else might be inside that a little coaching could bring out.

16. How to Give a Cat Its Medicine

Always be kind to those in distress.

—A Good Dad Adage

The cat is in pain and requires medicine. But whether it needs a teaspoon of mineral oil to ease its digestion or ear drops to banish mites, there's one thing for certain: the cat will object. If it's your kid's job to take care of the cat, he could get scratched or bitten in an honest attempt to help.

Fortunately, you know the way your child can give the cat its medicine and still do it safely. He simply needs to learn an age-old dad skill anybody can teach: the ability to wrap a cat.

First, lay a large towel across your child's lap. Then have him lay the cat on its side with its head just off the edge of the towel. The cat is a little mystified, but no flashing claws or bared teeth so far.

Now have your child take the cat's front legs and tuck them firmly back under its tummy. If he does this gently, the cat will still cooperate. Then, before the cat knows what's happening, *KA-PURR!* Your kid wraps the towel around the cat three or four times, nice and snug. Have him wrap the cat up like a mummy, with its body so locked up it can't move. And it's too late. He's got it. There the cat is, with its head sticking out of the towel like a baby peeking out of a blanket. It can't move. It can't do anything. It knows struggling is useless, so it lies perfectly still while your child administers the healing elixir.

This skill actually keeps both the cat and your kid safe. It also teaches your kid that sometimes being firm can be a very loving thing to do.

DAD TIP

How to Give a Cat a Pill

Once a cat's immobilized in the towel, it's easy to give it a pill. Simply grasp its head from above on both sides of its mouth where its jaws meet. Then press in with your finger and thumb until it opens wide. Tilt its head back. Now have your child drop the pill as far back on the cat's tongue as he can. He may want to use an unsharpened pencil to push the pill farther in the cat's mouth. Then have  him close the cat's mouth and stroke its throat until it swallows. To help the pill go down easier, he may want to smear it with a little butter.

17. How to Shinny Up a Tree

Victory is not won in miles but in inches. Win a little now, hold your ground, and later win a little more.

—Louis L'Amour, a Good Dad of Two

The word "shinny" isn't even in most unabridged dictionaries. Yet this technique of scooting up a tree trunk without the aid of a ladder or a chair has been a mainstay of dad knowledge for generations. Why? Because it teaches perseverance, a wonderful sense of self-reliance, and the rewards of getting ahead on your own strength. But it does require that your child wear a long-sleeved shirt and long pants, so the tree bark won't scrape up her arms and legs.

1. Have your kid wrap her arms and legs tightly around a tree trunk and hold on. If she's in a good shinnying position her knees will be slightly above her waist and her hands will be even with or above her head (figure a).

2. Now have her use her thighs and upper arms to lift herself higher (figure b).

3. As she holds tight with her legs (figure c), have her grab for a new position with her hands. In this new position, her hands will be even with or higher than her head.

4. Now as she holds tight with her arms, have her grab for a new position with her legs (figure d) and lock them around the trunk.

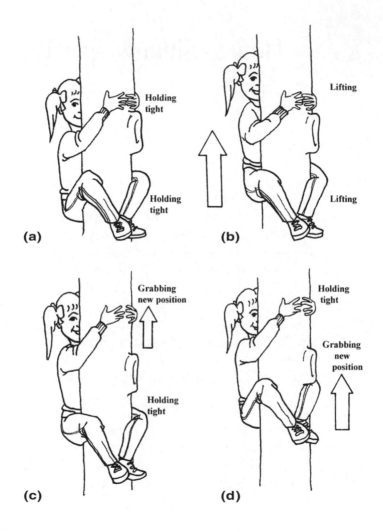

When she's shinnying correctly, she'll be slowly moving up the trunk like an inchworm.

Many ways of teaching children to rely on their physical strength will only make them more aggressive. But in all our searching, we found no crime nor hostile act ever recorded that was the end result of shinnying up a tree.

DAD SAFETY TIP

The first few times your child tries shinnying up a tree, you may want to provide her with a bicycle helmet and stand by in case she slips. To eliminate any chance of falls, you might even have her wear a safety harness attached to a rope passed over a high, sturdy limb. You can then hold onto the rope, taking up the slack as she climbs.

18. How to Find the Leak in a Flat Bicycle Tire

Finding the problem is half the solution.

—A Good Dad Maxim

It's a lame child who has a flat bicycle tire. And you can't always be there to fix the flat when it happens. Your kid can get kits from a bike shop to patch a hole in the tire. But what if the problem's a leaky valve, instead? And how does he find the hole to patch it?

The answer: use soap bubbles. Have your kid mix about half a teaspoon of liquid dish soap in a small bowl of water. Inflate the tire. Then, with a paintbrush, he should dab plenty of soapy water on the valve stem. If the valve's leaking, a small bubble will appear on it and grow as the air escapes into the bubble. If the bubble appears, that's good. Compared to a punctured tire, a valve stem is a lot easier and cheaper to repair. He may simply have to tighten the valve.

Even after fixing a leaky valve, he should still check the tire for holes. So have him liberally paint the whole tire with soapy water. If there's a leak, a soap bubble will suddenly appear over the hole and begin to grow. That's the spot he needs to patch.

All bike shops have tire-patching kits, complete with their own instructions. The first time your kid patches a flat, you can watch but let him do all the work. The next time, he's on his own.

Teaching a child how to find the leak in a flat makes him more self-reliant and that makes him more independent. Each of us has something special to do, a task or mission we can only find through independence. Giving him a way to find a leak in a bicycle tire is putting him on the path that leads to himself.

19. How to Make a Paper Boat

Organizing is what you do before you do something, so that when you do it, it's not all mixed up.
——A. A. Milne, the Good Dad of Winnie-the-Pooh

Cheap plastic boats are easy to buy. But the child who can make his own paper boat (no staples, no tape, no glue) can control his own fun. Though folding a single sheet of paper into a watertight craft can be tricky, here's a boat any child can make. And when the going gets confusing, there's a spot of blue to guide him out of the chaos.

The secret to success is step 5. He shouldn't skip this step until he's confident with the process.

1. Choose an 8½-by-11-inch piece of paper and have him fold it in half lengthwise, along line A-B, so that corners 1 and 2 fall on corners 3 and 4 (figure a).

2. Next, have him fold corners A and B along dotted lines to point X (figure b).

3. Fold edge up along dotted line C-D, and do the same on the other side. He'll have something that looks like a hat (figure c).

4. Open the bottom of the "hat" between corners 1&3 and 2&4 (figure c) until the 1&3 corner meets the 2&4 corner. Then press the paper flat (figure d).

5. With a blue magic marker or pen, color the corners as indicated (figure d). This important step will make things go a lot easier in a minute.

6. Next he should fold the colored corners along the dotted line X-X up to point Q (figure d). He should do the same on the other side. He then has figure e.

7. He now opens between X and X, the same way he did in step 4.

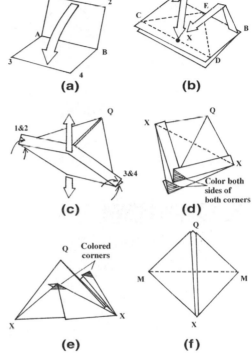

(a)

(b)

(c)

(d)

Color both sides of both corners

(e)

Colored corners

(f)

8. He now folds one point X along M-M up to Q (figure f). Then he flips the square over and folds the other point X along M-M up to Q.

Tell him to look down into the wads of folded paper. There, he'll see the two blue corners. When he pulls them in opposite directions, bingo! He has a boat that will impress all his friends. It's a good time for your child to learn that a plan is nothing but

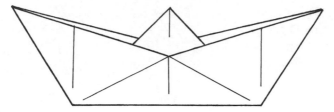

(g) The paper boat

foresight written down—and with foresight, he'll achieve amazing results.

DAD TIP

The Sailboat Plan

The classic design above creates a boat a bit like a battleship. If your child would rather have a sailboat, he can do this: In step 6 (figure d), instead of folding the colored corners all the way up to Q, he should fold them up halfway between line X and point Q. Then in step 8 (figure f), he should fold X (which now appears cut off) halfway between line M-M and point Q. When he pulls the boat open, it will have a higher "sail," and he'll have a sailboat.

---

20. How to Get a Cricket to Tell You the Temperature

We should all listen more than we talk. That's why God gave us two ears and one mouth.

—A Good Dad Adage

Children are great noise factories. Telling a child to be quiet is like telling Niagara Falls to stop falling. But there's one good way to get a child to stand still and listen. Teach him how to tell the temperature by a cricket's chirp.

The common snowy tree cricket—the one that makes the biggest racket on a warm summer night—sings by rubbing his front wings together. Female crickets don't chirp, but they do listen with tiny eardrums on their front legs. On a sultry evening, the snowy cricket chirps loudly and quickly. But as the temperature drops, his chirp becomes weaker and slower, until at about 55 degrees Fahrenheit, he stops singing completely.

Here's the secret way to translate those chirps into degrees Fahrenheit. Using a watch with a second hand, have your kid count the number of times the cricket chirps in 13 or 14 seconds. Then have him add 40. His answer will be the temperature in degrees Fahrenheit, give or take a degree. But, remember, this is the temperature around the cricket, who's probably out in the grass or under a rosebush. After a rainfall, when the ground's wet and moisture is evaporating, the cricket's hideaway is often cooler than the air around you. So he may be off a few degrees. But he'll still be accurate from his own perspective.

Which just goes to show that sometimes how you interpret the truth depends on where you're standing.

DAD FACTS

Cricket Truths and Legends

- Crickets are said to stop chirping when fairies go by. Crickets so greatly honor fairies that chirping in front of one would be like whistling in church.
- In the 1870s, it was recorded that a cricket ate a man's entire suit from pant cuffs to shoulder pads in a single night.
- Because of the cricket's fondness for gnawing on fur, the Cherokee Indians called this hungry little insect "talatu," meaning "barber."
- In many parts of the world, people eat crickets. Pound for pound, cricket meat is said to contain more protein than steak.

21. How to Coo through Your Hands

If you care enough, you'll give a hoot.

—A Good Dad Maxim

Though kids enjoy making rude noises, they also make charming sounds. They hum, sing, whistle, and coo. Coo? Yes. You know, that thing where you cup your hands, then blow into them and a cooing sound comes out?

The trick to learning how to coo is this: your kid really has to *want* to do it because it can't be taught. It can only be learned. Since each human hand is unique, your child will have to adjust his own musical "instrument" until he gets it just right. To get him started, however, you can pass along these timeless basics:

1. Make an airtight cavity with your hands. If there's even the tiniest air leak, no coo. Some people can coo by weaving their fingers together. But most of us need to cup our hands. Form a high, broad arch with the fingers of one hand (figure a). Then cup your hands together. When your hands are cupped right, the cavity inside them may look as if it were holding a small light bulb (figure b).

2. Form the "mouthpiece" (figure c) by placing your thumbs next to and parallel with each other, allowing only a sliver of space between them. Bend them slightly at the first joint.

3. Now blow short blasts of air down across your thumbs (not between them). To do this, put your lips right on the bend at the first joint. Your upper lip should rest on your thumbs above the joint, your lower lip against the straight part of your thumbs below the joint (figure d). Blow with about the same force you'd use when blowing on your cold hands to warm them in winter.

Tell your child it may take many hand adjustments to get it right. But once he masters this treasured skill, he'll have it for life. And each time he produces a coo, he'll remember the four cardinal rules of success: (1) try, (2) keep trying, (3) try again, and (4) repeat 1, 2, and 3.

Yet, sad to say, this is one of those endangered dad skills that's slowly but surely being lost. In 1799, Wordsworth said the hand coo was "known to most boys," although some were

---

DAD FACT

Ode to the Hand Coo

Hooting like an owl, or cooing like a dove through one's hands, is so charming that William Wordsworth, the good dad of Romantic poetry, once wrote a poem depicting a boy who could do it:

And there, with his fingers interwoven, both hands
Pressed closely palm to palm and to his mouth
Uplifted, he, as through an instrument,
Blew mimic hootings to the silent owls.

("There Was a Boy")

---

better at it than others. But with the Internet and all those Saturday morning cartoons, hand coo illiteracy is definitely on the rise. So good parents of the world, unite! We can still save this priceless skill before it's too late.

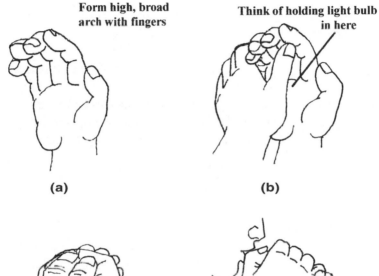

Form high, broad arch with fingers

Think of holding light bulb in here

(a)

(b)

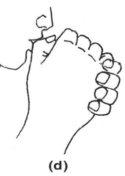

(c)

(d)

22. How to Make a Baby Laugh

When the first baby laughed for the first time, the laugh broke into a thousand pieces and they all went skipping about, and that was the beginning of fairies.

— J. M. Barrie, the Good Dad of Peter Pan

Every child loves being funny. Nothing makes a kid happier than making somebody else laugh. But since few kids really know how to tell a joke, their efforts often fall flat. Then they feel bad.

Fortunately, you know a way to make a baby brother or sister laugh every time that requires no comedic skills. Teach your kid this joke, and he'll have 'em laughing in the aisles, or at least giggling in their cribs.

Here's the joke: have your older kid open his eyes big and wide, lift his eyebrows high, and open his mouth in a big happy O. That's it. That's the joke. You think that's not funny? Sorry. Babies love it. They laugh and laugh at anybody who does it.

Your miniature comedian can build on the fun by adding sounds, such as an "ooooooooooooh" that increases in volume as he opens his mouth and eyes wider and wider. With this ever-popular baby joke, your kid can even make babies in the supermarket smile. And in the process, he'll have learned a valuable lesson: what's funny to one person may not be to another, but good cheer is a gift anybody can give.

DAD TIP

More Infant Thigh-Slappers

Here are two more baby "jokes" to teach your child.

Gonna get ya (also called gotcha): Have your child wriggle his finger in the air as he musically says, "IIIIIIIIIIIIIII-I'm gonna get ya." On the "gonna get ya," have him gently poke the baby's tummy with his finger. If the baby laughs, have him try the game again, with other variations (tickling the baby's tummy, circling his finger wide before poking the tummy, etc., etc.).

Tired horse: With his lips relaxed, have your child blow through his lips as a horse does when it's tired. Seven-month-olds find this especially hilarious. A good dad variation is to have your kid bury his face in the baby's stomach and do a tickling tired-horse lip flap.

23. How to Pick Up a Cat

Cats only understand one language, and we should all learn to speak it: the language of kindness.

—A Good Dad Maxim

Your kid looks at a cat and thinks, "Sure would like to pick up that cat. But there aren't any handles. Wait a minute. Maybe that's what those things are sticking out from his head." And so . . . well as you know, a cat handled incorrectly will scratch and bite to get free. And your child's relationship with that particular feline becomes forever soured.

So teach your child the right way to pick up a cat—and also the right way to hold it.

How to pick up a cat: Tell your child to support all parts of the cat's body. If he lets one leg or the cat's bottom dangle free, the animal will feel insecure and struggle. Your child should place one hand under the cat's stomach just behind her front legs and his other hand under the cat's hind quarters. Then he should lift the cat, supporting all her weight on the hand cupping her bottom. Use the same grip for a kitten, but be especially gentle because you can easily bruise a kitten's rib cage.

How to hold a cat: Now have your child lean the cat back against his body, supporting her with both arms. Many cats like being cradled upright, with their tummies facing out. But if the cat squirms or protests this position, try another. A good alternative is to have your child cuddle the cat gently like a baby, with her forepaws against his chest and her body supported by his arms.

By learning to pick up a kitten or cat correctly, your child will also be mastering another life lesson about charity toward others. It's called the Golden Rule, and it's always been the heart of loving.

DAD FACT

How Much Should a Kitten Be Handled?

Contrary to popular myth, handling a kitten won't stunt its personality or make it puny. In fact, kittens given extra attention in the first thirty days of their lives become extra capable. Their eyes open earlier, and their brains are more active. They're also more sociable, more curious, less easily irritated, and better at solving problems. All Siamese kittens are born without markings and only develop them as they age. But the more frequently Siamese kittens are handled, the earlier their markings develop. Like all living creatures, cats thrive on love. So encourage your kid to pet his cat. It's good for both of them.

24. How to Change a Tire on the Car

Give me a place to stand, and I can move the world.
        —Archimedes, the Good Dad of Mechanical Leverage

Most kids can't change a tire because they lack the muscle power to loosen the nuts and tighten them back. But, as you know, anyone who lacks brute strength can still change a flat. The secret is leverage. With a three-foot pipe that just fits over the lug wrench handle, your ten-year-old will soon be popping those nuts on and off with the ease of a six-foot, 200-pound mechanic.

Obviously, no ten-year-old should change a tire beside the highway because that's too dangerous. But just for the experience, she can do it in the driveway. Here's how:

1. First, have her make sure the ignition is off and the car is in park (if it's a manual transmission, in *reverse*). Before she starts changing the flat, she should use rocks to block the two wheels at the other end of the car (both front and back).

2. Have her take out the spare tire, wrench, jack, and three-foot pipe. Pry off the hubcap with the flat end of the wrench. Set the hubcap to one side to be used later as a "dish" to hold the nuts. With the pipe over the lug wrench handle, have her loosen each wheel nut one turn.

3. Tell her to check the car owner's manual to find the "jacking points" (the place where she should set the jack). Making sure the jack fits squarely under one of these "points," she can then jack up the car until the wheel is about two inches off the ground.

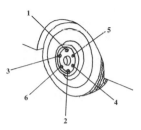

4. Now have her finish removing the nuts and put them in the hubcap so they won't get lost.

5. She should slide off the tire and replace it with the spare. Then starting at the top of the wheel first, have her replace the nuts in the order shown (see figure), tightening each with her fingers.

6. Lowering the car and removing the jack, she can now tighten the nuts with the wrench in the same order used in step 5. Have her repeat this tightening with the pipe on the wrench.

7. Last, she should replace the hubcap, snapping it in place with the heel of the hand, and then remove the rocks under the wheels.

Your child has just performed a mechanical feat worthy of a Goliath—all because she knew how to use leverage. Thanks to you and Archimedes, when she gets old enough to drive, she'll never be marooned on a back road.

25. How to Go to Bat

You are the first You in history. So don't try to copy anybody else's batting stance. Be yourself.

—Good Dad Axiom

Going to bat looks simple until a kid actually tries it in practice. Suddenly, he's told to stand close to the plate—but not too close. Swing hard—but not too hard. Keep his feet apart— but not too far apart. The kid spends so much time adjusting his position that he can't hit the ball.

But you know a better way to teach a kid how to go to bat. Long before spring practice begins, when he's at home and relaxed, you help him discover how to do it his way. When he picks up the bat in practice and that first pitch comes in, he already knows how to stand the way that's most natural for him.

To do this, chalk a home plate on the garage floor and hang a ball from the ceiling. Then show him how to grip the bat, with all eight fingers of both hands lined up in a row. Now show him where to stand at the plate, slightly in back of it so he can get a good long look at the ball. Also, show him how to measure how far he should stand from the plate by tapping the outside of the plate with his bat. He should stand so the end of the bat just reaches the outside edge of the plate.

Now hang a ball high and on the outside corner of the plate, so he can hit it over and over again. Then shift the ball around: high and inside, low and inside, low and outside. Have him work all the corners of the plate at all the different heights. Gradually, a stance will begin to emerge. Sure, he may have a funny coiled kind of stance, a little like the way Stan "the Man" Musial used to hit. He may hit the ball with authority only by striking out of a coil. You don't know why, but it works. He calls it his "cobra strike." But you know it's his natural stance because you were there watching when he developed it.

And day by day, as he steps up to that plate with authority, he'll become the kind of person who takes hold of life with authority. It's a little moment, but as a good dad once said, "Everyday men shape their lives with great moments; and great men, with everyday moments."

26. How to Use a Screwdriver

Man may not be the only animal that uses tools, but he is the only animal that takes good care of his tools

—"Rosie" Browder, a Good Dad of Six

To kids, a screwdriver looks invincible. So when a wagon handle gets loose or a toy truck falls apart, kids often seize any screwdriver that's handy and set to work—with disastrous results. Before long, the screw head's chewed up or sheared off, and the screwdriver's chipped or twisted, making it useless.

So before such a minor catastrophe occurs, teach your kid the dad rule anybody can teach: each screw requires the right screwdriver.

First, she must consider the *type* of screwdriver the job requires. Does she need a Phillips or a regular head? Does she need a screwdriver for wood or for metal? On a screwdriver for wood, the two faces of the blade are filed down parallel with each other. On a screwdriver designed for metal, the blade is wedge-shaped. If your kid uses the wrong screwdriver on a wood screw, the blade will slip out of the slot. Sometimes this problem can be eliminated by using soap to lubricate the screw so it's easier to turn. But it's best to use the correct tool.

Second, she must consider the *fit*. Teach her that for any screw, the screwdriver should fit exactly in the slot. The screwdriver blade should end right at the edge of the screw, with no overlap. If the screwdriver's too big, she can easily apply too much force and shear off the screw. If it's too small, it will chew up the slot and probably also damage the screwdriver.

Other than the extra time it takes to replace it, a damaged screw is of little consequence. But if she damages the screwdriver, she's lost an expensive tool and the time required to go buy a new one. Rosie Browder used to have another favorite saying that seems applicable here: "Take good care of your tools, and they'll take care of you."

DAD FACT

Is It a Phillips or Regular Head?

Make sure your child understands the difference between Phillips head and regular screws and screwdrivers. The regular head screw has the slot cut straight across the top. The Phillips head is usually cut in the shape of a cross. Each type requires its own special screwdriver.

27. How to Get a Boomerang to Come Back

There's no magic button on a boomerang.

—Good Dad Wisdom

The boomerang has been dubbed the most completely useless, most utterly satisfying invention of caveman minds for space-age thinkers. But a 'rang that doesn't return can make a kid feel like the world's worst failure. What's he doing wrong?

In reality, you know it's probably not the kid's fault. There's a big secret to getting a boomerang to come back: you have to buy one that will.

A surprising number of devices sold as "boomerangs" are secretly just useless sticks. They're so poorly designed that they'll never return. Those flexible plastic 'rangs sold in toy stores are especially bad news. They'll fly about ten feet through the air, then twist out of shape and flop out of the sky.

You can look for a good boomerang for a kid in a sporting-goods store or a kite shop. But the best beginners' boomerangs we found were available by mail order on the Internet. Price doesn't necessarily mean quality. We bought one useless stick for eighteen dollars in a kite shop, but a lovely little boomerang on the Internet for twelve dollars. Each arm of the 'rang should be shaped like the wing of an airplane, flat on one side, rounded on

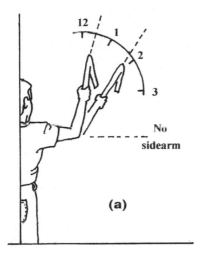

12 1 2 3

No sidearm

(a)

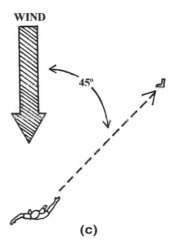

(b)

WIND

45°

(c)

73

the other. It should also be made of a rigid material. Plywood is good, but Styrofoam is also okay. If your kid is left-handed, be sure to buy a left-handed boomerang. There really is a difference.

The proof of the boomerang, though, is in the throwing. So take your kid to a wide-open spot like a park or field where there are no people, cars, or windows. Then have him practice throwing the 'rang at a slight angle (somewhere between twelve and two o'clock, as in figure a). He should never throw a boomerang side-armed like a Frisbee because it won't return and he could set up a dangerous flight pattern. When throwing, he should hold the 'rang by one tip with his thumb on the rounded side (figure b).

It's best to go boomeranging on a very calm day. But drop a few blades of grass to see if there's a wind. If there is, he should try to throw across the wind at a forty-five-degree angle (figure c). Have him throw with a smooth, hard motion and a snap of his wrist. He should aim at a spot slightly above the horizon. When he's throwing well, he won't even have to let go of the 'rang. It will just pop out of his hand.

Even a boomerang that works probably won't land directly at his feet on his first tries. But if it makes a clear turn and comes back in his vicinity, it's definitely working. Now he just has to work for accuracy.

There's a world apart from your child, a world that works independently of him and in which he has to make choices. Learning to buy a well-made boomerang and then learning to throw it well shows him that success is often a matter of making correct choices coupled with taking correct action.

28. How to Catch a Boomerang

There's a right and a wrong time to do everything.
—A Good Dad Adage

Even among the early Aborigines (who were quite playful), boomerangs were probably used only as toys. They weren't heavy enough to be weapons. Still, when a boomerang is caught wrong, it can hurt.

The secret is to wait for the right time. There's a time in the flight of the 'rang when it's picking time, when your child can reach out and pluck it out of the air as easily as picking a peach off the tree. This moment comes toward the end of its flight when the boomerang slows down, hovers, and drops as gently out of the sky as a maple seed.

Caution your child not to try to catch a 'rang until she knows its flight pattern. As she throws, have her notice that it begins its flight traveling fairly rapidly and spinning quickly as it climbs into the sky. Soon it shifts its trajectory and begins a great sweeping circle back to her, still spinning rapidly. No one should try to catch a boomerang when it's traveling like this.

As it completes its turn, it suddenly "lies down;" it shifts to a horizontal spin and begins to spin almost lazily. This is the right time to catch it. Tell her to make a boomerang sandwich with her hands as the bread and the 'rang as the meat. As it drops out of the sky, to about chest level, she should step forward, place one hand above the boomerang and one hand below it, with palms parallel to the boomerang. Then have her slap her hands together, like catching a mosquito. BAM! She's caught her boomerang.

As she grows up and years go by, she may be pursuing a promotion and remember that first time she captured a wooden bird between her hands. And she'll remember there's a right and a wrong time to do everything. She could make the right choice simply because you taught her how to wait under a boomerang and make her move at just the right moment.

29. How to Get a Cat Out of a Tree
(without Calling the Fire Department)

What goes up must come down—unless its claws are on backwards.
—A Good Dad Proverb

The cat's up a tree, mewing piteously, and the kids are going berserk. The poor kitty! It looks so hungry and scared. How will it ever get down? Reassuring common sense—"It'll get down. Have you ever seen a cat skeleton in a tree?"—merely falls on deaf ears. And the thought of carrying a terrified feline under one arm down a ladder doesn't strike you as sane, either.

Fortunately, you can avert this crisis before it even crops up. In fact, that's the only way you can avert it. Before the cat ever gets stuck, you have to teach it to climb *down* a tree.

A cat can only climb down a tree backward, tail first. Why? Because its claws are curved back toward its tail. If it tries descending head-first, it can't get a grip. It'll fall. Unfortunately, the cat only becomes aware of this problem after it's scaled to a lofty height. It suddenly realizes it's stuck, and there's not a darned thing it can do about it.

So, long before your family pet gets itself in such a pickle, give it "cat power;" teach it how to get out of a tree.

Put the cat up on a low branch. Then guide it back down the tree trunk until it's got it. Or, if you have an older cat, enlist help. There's a story—absolutely true—about a cat that couldn't get out of a tree. The kids had tried all day to get the poor kitty down. Bowls of its favorite food set at the base of the tree got no results. The cat just sat up there and thought about the nature of the universe and the shape of its claws. Then cat #2 came along. This was an experienced tree-climber. It scurried up the tree and rapidly climbed down. Cat #1 watched curiously but didn't budge. Cat #2 performed its neat trick again.

Cat #1 sat as if dumbfounded. Finally, the third time was the charm. When Cat #2 once again descended the tree, its protégée dutifully followed it down.

Teaching the family cat to get out of a tree will delight your kids while also teaching a valuable lesson: avoid problems, kids, by looking ahead. Your claws might be bent wrong.

30. How to Tie a Really Fast Knot

There's a right way and a wrong way to do everything. And it doesn't take any longer to do it the right way.

—Floyd Hurdle, a Good Dad of Three

Tying any knot can be a real labor for children. In most cases, they'll worry the knot into existence, checking and rechecking each twist and loop. By learning to tie one knot really fast, your child will be challenged to work faster in other areas.

How fast can he tie this knot? As quickly as he can put his hands together and take them apart. The secret: he needs to use his two middle fingers as hooks. Just for the record, this is a two-way mast hitch, originally used by sailors to hold two masts together.

1. Have him start with the rope held loosely (figure a). His hands should be about two or three feet apart, right palm turned away from him, left palm turned toward him. When he's holding the rope right, both thumbs will point in the same direction, as shown.

2. Now have him bring his palms together, making one loop in the rope.

3. He should then make a hook out of each middle finger. Now with his right middle finger, he catches the rope where it trails below his left hand. At the same time, with his left middle finger, he catches the rope where it emerges from the top of his right hand (figure b).

4. Holding the rope with only his two middle fingers, he snaps his hands apart, and the rope instantly tightens into a knot (figure c). And there it is! The two-way mast hitch (figure d).

With a little practice, he can now tie a knot as fast as he can clap his hands. And each time he does, he'll remember the key to success nowadays isn't just what you know. It's also how fast you know it.

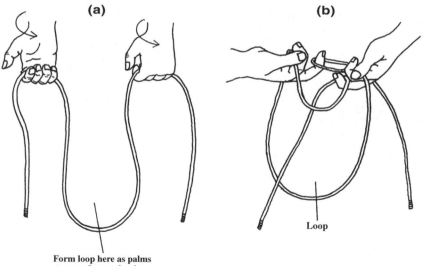

(a)

Form loop here as palms
turn to face each other

(b)

Loop

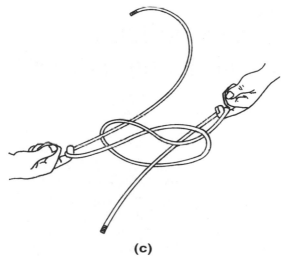

(c)

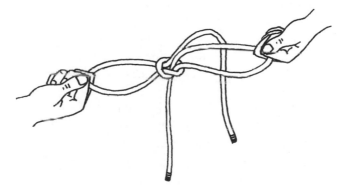

(d) A really fast knot

31. How to Tell a Moth from a Butterfly

Always stay alert and pay attention to details.
— A Good Dad Motto

To a child, a butterfly resembles a fairy. Flitting from flower to flower, feasting first on red, then on blue, this gossamer-winged nymph calls up images of Peter Pan's Tinkerbell. Then, just when a kid thinks she's got the butterfly's I.D. down pat, somebody says, "That's not a butterfly . . . that's a moth." Huh? What's the difference? Confusion buzzes in the kid's brain. A little of the fun just went out of butterflies.

Fortunately, your kid won't stay baffled long, because you know the easiest way to tell a moth from a butterfly: simply look at the creature's antennae. A butterfly has a long, smooth, wire-like antenna with a knob on the end. A moth's antennae are furry or feathery. Some moths' feelers are so fuzzy they look like baby bird feathers.

Your kid can also tell moths from butterflies by the way they rest on a bush. A butterfly sits with its wings upright. A moth sits more with its wings folded down.

By learning to tell a moth from a butterfly, your kid will gain a new understanding of nature and more confidence in her observations. She'll also learn that big differences are often found in small places. Always read the fine print.

DAD TIP

How to Watch Moths Up Close

It's easy to attract lots of moths at night by turning on the porch light. But how do you observe moths acting naturally (not just banging their heads against a light bulb)? Here's a great way to study those little buggers so they won't even know you're there. Have your kid paint a tree trunk with a mixture of beer and molasses. Then cover a flashlight with red cellophane (moths can't see a  red light) and wait until dark. The moths will come to feed on the stinky, sweet "sap," and your child can study them under the red light to her heart's content.

32. How to Give Your Kid a Star

The stars are eternal, unobtainable, and a great call to noble adventure. Every kid should own one.

—Dad Reflection

Kids are far removed from the heavens anymore. What with homework, television, and the Internet, the silent stars get little attention. A child can go his whole childhood without hearing a star called by name. So make your child feel that one little corner of the heavens belongs to him. Give him a star.

We don't mean buy him one. We're not talking about those offers in the back pages of astronomy magazines where you can pay money to have a star named after him. He can't see that star. It won't mean a thing. We mean *give* him one of the stars in the night sky—for free.

Pick it out especially for him. Maybe he's particularly intelligent, so you choose Sirius because it's the brightest star in the sky. Maybe the night he was born you looked out the window and saw one bright light in the sky, overwhelming all the stars there. Remember which star that was. Give it to him as a present. Go out

of your way to learn facts and stories about that star. Then tell them to him.

If you're an amateur astronomer, this will be particularly easy. If not, you might want to ask at a library reference desk for books about stars. Learn all about his star. Then spend an evening outside with your child looking at the sky and telling him everything you've learned. That's his star. From this night on, whenever he gazes up at the night sky, he'll think about his star. And since he can see this star from many points on earth, he'll be able to find it even in far countries.

Who knows what great things might be expected from someone who owns a piece of the heavens?

33. How to Walk on Stilts

Some people march to a different drummer—and some walk on stilts.
—A Good Dad Saying

Kids are lightweight shorties, and don't think they haven't noticed. How splendid it would be if they could suddenly sprout two or three feet. Well, your kid can do exactly that. On a pair of stilts, for a few minutes each day, any kid can look down on the biggest adult.

So build your kid a pair of stilts. Build them as tall as she'd like. Then teach her the secret to walking on them. Which is? She has to hold them tight against the soles of her shoes so they're like extensions of her legs. Some kids get so good on stilts they can even skip rope.

Stilts are just two long poles with small platforms attached. You can make them of any material that will support your child's weight. But wooden two-by-twos work well. Cut off two pieces of two-by-fours about six inches long for the little platforms. Bolt each platform to a two-by-two, using a bolt one-quarter inch in diameter and seven inches long (see figure). Your kid wants to be two feet taller? Bolt the platforms two feet from the ends of the stilts (see figure). She wants to be three feet taller? Fine. Put the platforms three feet from the ends.

The tops of the stilts should be long enough to extend above her shoulders. If they're not and she slips off, the tops of the stilts could catch her under the armpits. But if they extend above her shoulders, this won't happen. Sand down the stilts so she won't get splinters.

Now have her stand on a car bumper, fence, or step that's as high as the little platforms on the stilts. Then as she holds the stilts, have her step out on the platforms and walk away. Be sure

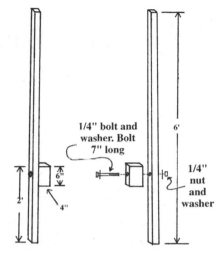

she keeps her arms at her sides and pulls up on the stilts, holding them tight against the soles of her shoes. For balance, the tops of the stilts should be *behind* her shoulders. At first, you may have to catch her whenever she starts to fall. But soon she'll be walking around the yard, towering over bushes, striding lordly among the trees. Man! It's great to be tall.

Eventually, though, she'll come to realize being big isn't so special. She still has all the same problems she had before. Being tall hasn't made her homework one bit easier nor won her any new friends. It's just another vantage point from which to view the world. No better. No worse. Just different. People have scrambled and fought and climbed a lot farther than two or three feet to learn that.

34. How to Build a Snow Candle

When the world has grown dark and cold, light a candle.
                                                —A Good Dad Maxim

The year's first snowfall is usually skimpy. There's just not enough white stuff for a snowman or a fort. Yet kids still want to build something.

So is this a problem? Not! You know how to build an enchanting structure of fire and snow that will enthrall your kid for hours—a snow candle. In fact, you're going to build several of them and line them up on both sides of the driveway. By the time you get done, your driveway will look like an O'Hare International runway at night.

First, work with your child to make a bunch of snowballs. Place seven or eight of the larger balls in a circle to lay a "foundation." Then using the other snowballs like bricks, build a wall three or four snowballs high (see figure). With each layer of snowballs, slant the wall slightly inward—toward the center of the circle. Put plenty of little holes between the snowballs, so heat can escape and your "candle" won't melt so fast. Keep arching the wall inward, building a small igloo. Although the walls lean at an angle, they won't collapse because the pressure from the arch holds them up.

At the very top of the tiny igloo, show your child how to leave a hole just large enough for your hand. Now take a real wax candle, set it down inside the house, and light it. Then cap off the house with one last snowball. It should be about sunset, and the snow candle will glow warm and golden in the evening light.

The snow candle will eventually melt, but your child can still enjoy the lovely memory of its glowing presence. Creations that lift our hearts and bring us joy, no matter how brief, have always been candles against the dark.

35. How to Oil a Bicycle, Wagon, or Anything Else That Needs It

Oil is like politeness in a social setting. Used moderately it lets us work together without overheating.

—A Good Dad Observation

Any kid who's seen *The Wizard of Oz* will love learning about oil. Just remind him of that can the tin man always carried around. No kid can resist the delightful metallic *onk-onk* sound of the oilcan in action. But too much oil is a bad thing.

The secret is for him to learn to go *onk-onk . . . onk-onk,* using just a little oil at a time. Most kids get carried away with a rapid-fire *onka-onka-onka-onka-onka* that leaves oil dripping sloppily all over the place. When they finish oiling their bikes and go pedaling down the street, they look like they're being chased by a rainstorm of petroleum. So show your kid how to use just the right amount of oil (not too little, not too much). Teach him how to use an oilcan correctly.

First, show him the long, thin spout on the can, through which small amounts of oil can be released. Then show him how to dispense oil a drop at a time by pushing on the thumb-operated pump, the slightly concave bottom, or the side of the can.

Your child can tell he's used enough oil when the metal gets slightly darker. If the metal is shiny or the oil runs off in a stream, he's used too much. Once he's squirted on a few drops of oil, have him move the part for a few seconds. A well-oiled part runs smoothly, without overheating. It even runs more quietly.

Too much oil, and the moving part will throw off oil everywhere, fouling whatever's near—maybe your child. Too little, and he may damage the part. But there is a small happy application that makes everything work fine, and that's why the oilcan was invented. Oil on machinery is a lot like manners in our social lives—too few manners and you have a grouch; too many and you have a toady. Temperance solves the problem, and the oilcan is temperance in action.

36. How to Tie a Bow Tie

There are some things you just won't do in a bow tie. That's why you wear one.

—A Good Dad Saying

Since business suits require neckties, most kids learn only to tie neckties. But a tux calls for a gentlemanly bow. And you certainly don't want your offspring reduced to wearing a clip-on when he walks onstage to accept the Nobel Prize. So prepare him now for his Inaugural Ball, the Oscars, or at least his senior prom. Teach him how to tie a bow tie.

This nearly lost dad skill can take time to learn, so allow at least half an hour for the first try. (If your kid can master it in under twenty minutes, he's a genius.) But here's how to perform this dad feat in six simple steps:

1. Have him drape the tie around his neck. Let left end A hang lower than right end B.

2. Run A over B, back under B, and up past the neck and through the loop at the neck (figure a). Both ends should now be the same length. (If they're not, adjust them until they are.) Have him feel with his index finger until he finds Little Loop Q on the backside of the knot and at his throat. Loop Q will be really important in a minute.

3. Now have him lay end A back over his left shoulder to get it out of the way. Then have him form the left side of the

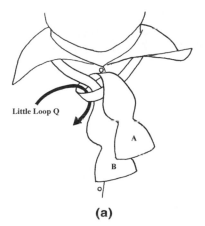

Little Loop Q

(a)

bow by doubling up end B and placing it across his collar points (figure b). Tell him to hold the left side of the bow with his left index and middle fingers and keep the tie snug against his neck, but not so tight that Little Loop Q is lost. (This is an art, not a science.)

4. With his right hand, have him pull end A so it hangs down over B.

5. Now have him place his right forefinger, pointing up, on the bottom half of A, pass A up under B (figure c), and poke A to his right through Little Loop Q.

6. Finally, have him pull both big loops, adjusting the bow until it looks great (figure d). If the bow *doesn't* look great, he'll just have to try again.

Tying a bow tie isn't like learning to microwave a TV dinner. The six steps to perfection require more work than pushing a few buttons. But as your child struggles to create a classic silk bow, just remind him a good dad once

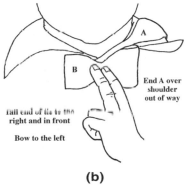

A

B

End A over shoulder out of way

fat end of tie to the right and in front

Bow to the left

(b)

said it's easier to be a hero than a gentleman. As he twists, turns, tugs, and finally gets it right, he'll also begin to understand that elegance and good manners aren't inborn; they're the result of diligent effort.

(c)

(d)

37. How to Throw a Frisbee

If we all completely became whatever a skill teaches, Frisbee throwers would turn into graceful swans.

—A Good Dad Observation

Your kid wants to play catch with a Frisbee. But each time she hurls the disk your direction, it wobbles in the air, then veers off course and crashes into a rosebush.

Fortunately, you know the secret that will blitz her frustration and help her make those long, hovering throws of her dreams: it's all in the wrist action.

First, have her grasp the Frisbee, placing the four fingers of her throwing hand under the rim and her thumb on top. When she curls her arm in toward her body, her thumb should point right at her chest. Then have her rapidly uncurl her arm and let the Frisbee go with a quick snap of her wrist when her hand points at the receiver. By flicking the wrist, she puts spin on the disk, which makes it work like a top. This keeps it stable so it doesn't tilt.

For a longer, more hovering throw, have her aim toward you, but also slightly above the horizon. As the air flows over the Frisbee, it will act like an airplane wing, rising higher and staying aloft longer. If she wants more power to her toss, have her run a few steps before her release. Soon she'll be making smooth, graceful throws that will sail clear across a field.

Catching a Frisbee is simple. As it spins in her direction, just have her reach out and catch it by the rim. Remind her to clutch it firmly because it will be spinning.

Your child will learn that like ballet or playing the violin, throwing the Frisbee is a skill that requires correct patterns of behavior. And the slow, gentle way of Frisbee throwing, with its display of elegance and grace, is a good pattern to learn.

DAD TIP

A "Look-at-This!" Catch

For more razzmatazz to her catches, your kid can work to perfect the supercool "rolling catch," in which she makes the Frisbee appear to roll across her body. Let's say the Frisbee is coming in from her left. Simply have her let the Frisbee graze her extended left hand, roll down her left arm, spin across her chest, and roll up her right arm. Then with her right hand, have her pluck the disk out of the air.

38. How to Head a Soccer Ball

You should always be timid about being too timid.

—A Good Dad Motto

Kids watch pro soccer players hitting 40 mph balls with their heads and think, "Wow! How can I bang a goal home with my head?" It all seems so incredibly cool. But you know heading a soccer ball is a skill developed over time. A child should not try to hit a fast-moving soccer ball with his head. But even with a slow-moving one, a kid can fear getting hit and close his eyes or flinch when the ball comes his way—reactions that increase the odds that he'll get hurt.

Before any child starts heading soccer balls, he should learn the secret all the pros know. He should hit the ball only with his forehead. There's a lot of flat area there to absorb the blow, so he won't get hurt. That's also how he'll gain most control.

But until he gets his accuracy down, he should practice with something soft—like a big beach ball. Have him put a cross of tape on his forehead and practice hitting the ball on that spot until he can do it accurately every time.

Once he changes to a soccer ball, he must head the ball with boldness, but not foolish boldness. He should still bend his knees slightly to lessen the blow. And you should teach him to always keep his mouth closed (so he won't bite his tongue). He must also learn to keep his eyes open (so he can see where he's aiming the ball). When a ball comes toward a kid's head, he just naturally tends to shut his eyes tight. Boldness will keep his eyes open.

He might also tie a soccer ball from a tree limb in the backyard, so he can practice keeping his eyes open when he jumps up and bangs it with his forehead. This will help him a lot with high balls on the field.

Learning to head a soccer ball teaches skill, coordination, and a wonderful combination of courage and prudence. Where else can you convince a kid it's a good idea to keep his eyes open and his mouth shut?

39. How to Throw a Baseball

Always stand straight, sit straight, act straight, talk straight, and throw straight.

—A Good Dad Adage

In 1935, a line drive hit the great pitcher Dizzy Dean on the toe. It hurt his throwing arm so much it ended his career. How did a baseball hitting a man's toe injure his throwing arm?

There's a secret hidden in the answer that will help your kid throw a baseball correctly. He doesn't just throw with his arm; he throws with his whole body. As your child learns to throw with his body, he'll get more power in his throws and have greater control. He'll also be less apt to get hurt.

But before you teach him to throw, he first needs to understand a few terms. If he's right-handed, he should think of his whole right side as his "throwing side." Therefore, he doesn't just have a throwing arm; he also has a throwing shoulder and a throwing foot. If he's left-handed, his left side is his throwing side.

Now to begin the lesson, first show your child how to point his non-throwing shoulder at his target. Have him pull his throwing arm behind and slightly above his head and throwing shoulder. As he does this, he should rotate his upper body so that a line drawn through both shoulders will point directly at the target.

Have him solidly plant his throwing foot. He might even want to stomp the ground a little. Then have him take one stride forward with his non-throwing foot, pointing his toes at the target. As he does this, he should also rotate his upper body ninety degrees so he's squarely facing the target, bring his throwing arm forward and down, and drive hard with his throwing leg. He'll generate power with that leg. The harder he drives, the faster he'll throw. When his throwing shoulder points directly at the target, he lets the ball go, driving hard with his throwing leg. And *ka-whoosh!* The ball rockets across the field and explodes in the fielder's glove.

As your child learns to throw a baseball with power, he's also learning the power of self-control. Day by day, we build our character the same way we learn to throw a baseball—with practice and self-discipline.

40. How to Tie Four Really Handy Knots

A knot is a rope's independence. It can achieve whatever it sets out to do by fashioning a solution out of itself.

—A Good Dad Observation

When a child wants to tie her puppy to a long leash or hang a baseball in the garage for batting practice, she'll often use a slip knot or a granny knot. The first is dangerous for the dog, and the second can wind up so jammed it has to be cut.

A kid doesn't realize that different knots have been designed over centuries for different uses. To choose the right knot, your child simply needs to ask, "How will I be using this rope?"

Here are four knots and what they do best.

Square knot (figure a.5): This knot works best for tying two loose ends of the same rope tightly together, as when wrapping a package. It can tolerate light to moderate tension. But under too much tension, it can slip. The square knot is probably the easiest of all knots to tie. Just tell your kid to follow the arrows in

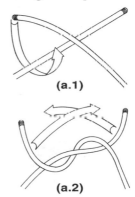

(a.1)

(a.2)

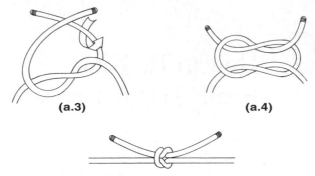

(a.3)   **(a.4)**

(a.5) Square knot

figures a.1 to a.4 and remember right over left and left over right.

Sheet bend (figure b.4): Used to attach a thinner line to a thicker one. Your kid can use this knot anytime she has two short ropes of different thicknesses she wants to tie into one long rope, such as when she's tying a Christmas tree to the top of the car.

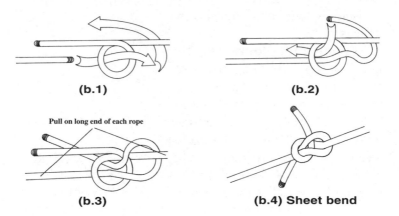

(b.1)   **(b.2)**

Pull on long end of each rope

(b.3)   **(b.4) Sheet bend**

Bowline (figure c.4): A very reliable knot. It won't slip or jam and is easy to untie even when the rope is wet. Have your kid use this knot when there will be lots of tension on a rope, yet only one end can be fastened in place, such as when tying a dog on a long leash. Just look at the illustrations and follow the arrows.

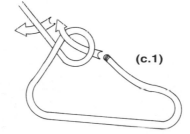

(c.1)

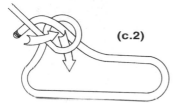

(c.2)

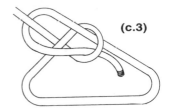

(c.3)

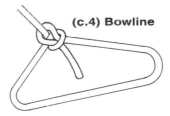

(c.4) Bowline

Round turn and two half hitches (figure d.3): A quick tie that works very well when fastening a small hanging object in place. Good for tying a baseball to a rafter in the garage.

With just these four knots, your kid will be well on her way to learning how to use a rope properly. But as you pass on these knot-tying basics, you're also passing on to your child the knowledge that each task in life has its own unique solution, and it's up to her to find it.

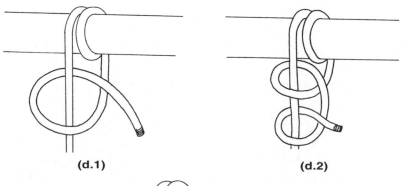

(d.1)   **(d.2)**

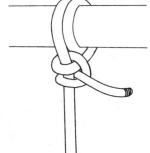

(d.3) Round turn and two half hitches

41. How to Pick Up a Bug without Using Your Hands

A big guy should never hurt a little guy.

—A Good Dad Motto

At one time or another, every child will feel the calling to pick up a bug. But there's double trouble. Robust bugs like some centipedes might bite or sting. Fragile bugs like the crane fly are easy to harm.

So how can your kid pick up a bug without endangering himself or the insect? Simple. Use a "pooter." It's cheap and easy to make. Yet it will protect him from any bug, while leaving the most fragile insect unscathed.

A pooter uses suction to pick up a bug. It works much like a vacuum cleaner, except it needs no electricity and has no moving parts to repair. Here's how your child can make a small pooter out of a bottle, a cork or rubber stopper, and two pieces of tubing.

Have him start with a wide-mouthed plastic or glass bottle. Into the mouth of this bottle, insert a rubber stopper with two holes in it. Then insert a tube into each hole. The tubes should just stick into the bottle. The other ends of the tubes hang loose under the bottle like octopuses' legs, as in the figure.

Now when your child wants to pick up a bug, have him put the end of Tube 2 over the bug and suck air through Tube 1. For a more elegant pooter, you can insert a syringe into the end of Tube 1. When your kid spots a bug, he squeezes the syringe. Then he puts Tube 2 over the bug and lets the syringe go. He'll draw the bug right into the bottle.

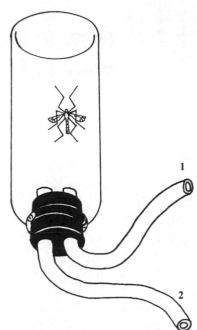

You can build a bigger pooter—one big enough to catch large grasshoppers and crickets—by using one large tube on an inflating pump for a basketball or a soccer ball.

By going to all this trouble to build a pooter, you're sending your child a gentle message: small, fragile lives should never be harmed. He who breaks a thing to find out what it is has left the path of wisdom.

42.

How to Pick Out a Good Puppy

The dog you get, is the puppy you buy.

—A Good Dad Proverb

When a child picks out a puppy, she'll pick the one that's cutest or wriggles most. But you know she'll have this puppy for years, and the dog's personality won't change. What your child really wants is a great grown-up dog.

So here are a few quick, easy tests your child can give any puppy to see how it will mature:

1. First, have her watch all the puppies in the litter for a few minutes to see how they interact with each other. Is one puppy a bully, while another acts timid and withdrawn? She should look for a confident puppy who holds his own without showing too much aggression.

2. Now have her take an object that has her scent on it, like an old glove or scarf, and toss it into the litter. See how the puppies react. The puppy who gains control of it is the dominant one and may be quite feisty as an adult. The puppy who shies or runs away from the glove is too timid and won't be fun to play with.

3. As the puppies are eating, have her make a loud noise, such as clapping her hands or suddenly jingling your car keys.

The well-balanced pup will perk up his ears or look to see where the noise came from and then go on eating. The dog that bolts is too timid.

4. Once she's spotted those puppies that seem most well-adjusted, have her pick out one of them and turn it on his back. If he lies there happily and likes being petted, he's an even-tempered dog that will like being handled. He should also be easy to discipline.

5. Finally, have her put her hands gently around the dog's neck. If the puppy growls, barks, or struggles to get away, he's very dominant and will be hard to train. On the other hand, if he goes limp, acts terrified, or recoils from her touch, he's overly submissive. You want the puppy that nonchalantly accepts her touch and seems quite content.

By following these guidelines, your child will choose a good puppy. But she'll also have learned that you can predict personalities, in dogs or in humans, by watching how someone acts in a group. And that's a good skill for any kid to know.

43. How to Pop a Wheelie

Difficulties vanish when faced boldly.
> —Isaac Asimov, a Good Dad of Science Fiction

At the circus, nobody has more fun than the clown riding a unicycle around the ring. And in your neighborhood, nobody will have more fun on his bike than the kid who can pop a wheelie. But this classic dad skill can be a dangerous stunt if a kid does it wrong.

So teach your kid how to pop a wheelie—safely. Most kids think they have to be pedaling down the street pell-mell at 100 mph to perform this impressive feat. But, in fact, you know that with good balance a kid can learn to pop a wheelie almost at a standstill.

The secret is for your kid to raise the front wheel of his bike until his body's center of gravity (approximately at his stomach) is directly above the spot where the back wheel touches the ground. Then he stops. If he can stay balanced, he's done a wheelie. A wheelie requires the same sense of balance a kid uses at a stoplight, when he hesitates just a moment without letting his foot touch the ground.

To teach your child this skill, find an unbumpy, empty stretch of sidewalk. (Make sure he's wearing his bicycle helmet.) Tell him not to go too fast. Slow is good. As he pedals along the walk, have him suddenly accelerate and at the same time yank back on his handlebars. As the front wheel raises, he should lean slightly forward, keeping his body aligned with the rear wheel.

If he yanks too lightly, the front wheel will rise only a few inches, then drop back to the ground. No problem. He can just try again. If he accelerates too fast and yanks on the handlebars too forcefully, he may begin to topple over backwards. That's okay, too. Simply have him drop his feet to the ground and catch himself (this is one reason he's going slow). Eventually, with practice, he'll gain confidence and be able to ride half a block on only his rear wheel.

A kid who can pop a wheelie appears to be a real daredevil to those who fear taking risks. But your kid will have learned that what looks bold and daring to more timid souls can often be a smart risk if he has the right skills.

44. How to Receive a Soccer Ball

Soccer is like good negotiating—the smart players know when to give a little.

—A Good Dad Reflection

When kids first take up soccer, kicking and passing look easy. But how does anybody control the ball? When kids watch other players, the ball just seems to bounce helter-skelter off all parts of their bodies.

To receive a soccer ball cleanly, your kid needs to learn how to "give" with his body. Then the ball will fall gently to his feet, where he can control it.

Depending on how high the ball comes to him, your kid can receive or "trap" the ball with his chest, thigh, or foot. But in all three cases, he needs to develop techniques that will allow his body to "give," or move slightly away from the ball at the moment of contact.

The chest trap: This trap is used for high-kicked and high-bouncing balls. When he starts practicing the chest trap, his first impulse will be to catch the ball with his hands. That's against the rules. So have him pick up a small rock or a handful of grass to hold. As the ball approaches, he should pull back his arms and stick out his chest. Then at the moment the ball impacts, he should pull his chest back and swing his arms forward. This is the "give," and the ball should drop at his feet.

The thigh trap: This is commonly used for falling balls. Have him raise his leg and prepare to receive the ball on his thigh. He should not bend his knee. As the ball hits, he should drop his leg (the "give"). The ball will bounce up, then fall dead at his feet. Now he can dribble, pass to another player, or maybe even kick a goal.

The foot trap: Used for rolling balls, this trap can be done with the sole, the instep, or the outside of the foot. As the ball approaches, your kid extends his trapping foot with his heel slightly above the ground, toe pointed up. Then as the ball hits his sole, he pulls his leg slightly back (the "give"). To use the instep or the outside of the foot, he lifts his foot about three inches off the ground. When the ball hits the foot, he should then cushion it by moving his foot slightly back.

Learning how to receive well helps your kid make both him and his teammate who passed the ball look good. And performing well in a way that also makes others look good is crucial, whether he's a kid working with a teammate on the soccer field or an adult later in life negotiating a business deal.

45. How to Pick Up a Lobster

A brave kid is afraid of a lobster three times: when he first looks it in the eye, when he first sees its claws, and when he first picks it up.
—A Good Dad Saying

Kids are fascinated by any geeky creature that moves. And the lobster with its eyes on stalks and slow-motion gait is the undisputed geek of the sea. One day you stop by one of those beach restaurants where you can pick out your own lobster for dinner. Your kid cautiously eyes all those shelled monsters in the tank and wonders if he could pick up one.

Is it safe? With you by his side, absolutely. The secret? Just grab him by that big, old, hard shell.

It's true lobsters have two strong claws that can crush and pinch. But most lobsters in restaurants and supermarkets have their claws banded closed. Even if the lobster's claws are free, he becomes immobilized when he's seized by his shell. He can't get around to snap.

Besides, a lobster is cold-blooded like a snake and moves slowest when he's cold. So a lobster in icy-cold water will be a pretty sluggish guy.

You child should come in behind the lobster and quickly seize him from above by that hard shell just where the lobster's last two legs join his tail. He may want to hold him down with one hand until he can get a firm grip with the other. Tell him to expect some resistance. Lobsters are stronger than they look.

By letting your kid pick up a lobster, you're giving him an exciting experience he can tell all his friends about. But you're also teaching him not to be timid. Later in life, he'll realize that, at first glance, something might seem fiercely unapproachable (a hostile office supervisor, for example) but he can handle it comfortably if he just knows how to go about it.

DAD FACTS

- When a lobster grows, he sheds his old shell and grows a new one. This is called molting. A newly molted lobster feels a lot like a Gumby.
- A grown lobster may look big and scary. But he starts life as an egg no bigger than a pinhead.
- A lobster may molt up to twenty-five times before he's five years old. After he molts, he has to hide for a week or two to keep from being eaten by a codfish or other predator while his new shell hardens.
- Live lobsters are usually the color you see in the fish market—greenish-black on top and orange underneath. But a few rare ones—one in every three or four million—are blue.

---

46. How to Build a Snow Fort

At first a baby is simply a small animal that eats and sleeps, but there will come a time when he will want to build a shelter.

—Louis L'Amour, the Good Dad of the Frontier Novel

Most kids think you only need snow to build a snow fort. But a good dad who's built many an icy rampart in the winters of his youth knows just any snowfall won't work. Snow that's too dry is powdery and unpackable. It will just fall to snow dust in your kid's hands. Snow that's too wet is like slush. Still, a day will come when you know a polar bulwark can go up. You wait. Your kid gets edgy. No. Not yet.

Then the day arrives, sunny, almost warm. You've seen days like this before. It's too clear. There's a storm coming. Tomorrow, winter will return with a vengeance. And you look at her and say, "Now!"

You knew that to build a snow fort right, you had to wait for a warm day right before a cold snap, so her hard work today wouldn't just be a puddle by morning.

First, show your kid how to start building her fort with big snow boulders (the kind she'd use for a snowman). Have her pile the big balls alternately on top of each other like bricks until she builds four high walls. It's important for her to pack the snow down hard, kind of whacking it with her hand until it's solid. Also, have her pack loose snow nice and tight into all the cracks to keep the wind out of her building. By doing this, she's making the fort stronger and warmer.

Once she has a fort started, her imagination can flow. Would she like a window? POW! with her fist. There's a window. Would she like a ladder to climb up the walls? Show her how to kick little indents into the wall with her toe, then scrunch the snow down hard with her foot to create a "step." Would she like flags on the parapets? What about that old scarf in the hall closet?

As she plays with her friends in the fort over the next several days, she'll have plenty of time to think about what she's learned. It's not always enough to know *how* to succeed. You also need to know *when* to act. Sometimes success is a matter of timing.

47. How to Tell Time by the Stars

The big clock in the sky is an hourly reminder that Earth and sky are part of the same universal bucket.

—A Good Dad Insight

Good dads teach skills that stretch kids' abilities to cope in the world. But they also teach attitudes that stretch kids' minds. This ageless dad skill—telling time by the stars—gives a child a bigger awareness of time, so he won't be mindlessly driven by life's smaller clocks.

First, take your kid out under the heavens and explain that the earth turns on its axis once every 24 hours.

Second, show him how to find the clock in the sky. He should already know how to find the North Star (see chapter 14). So he's halfway there. The North Star is the center of the clock. Now, as he gazes at the North Star, have him draw an imaginary line out through Dubhe and Merak, the pointer stars in the Big Dipper. This straight line is the hour hand of the clock (there is no minute hand). This hour hand makes a complete circle around the North Star every 24 hours.

Third, tell him the secret of this clock: at midnight on March 1, the hour hand points directly to midnight (straight up). When this hour hand moves, it moves counterclockwise (see

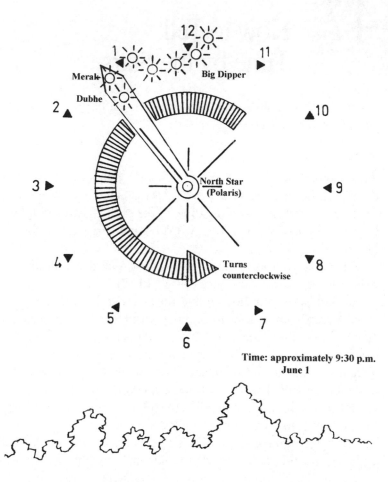

Merak

Dubhe

Big Dipper

North Star
(Polaris)

Turns
counterclockwise

Time: approximately 9:30 p.m.
June 1

figure). He should think of the numbers on the illustration as "markers." Each marker represents 2 hours. Marker #1 on the illustration indicates 2 hours past midnight; marker #2, 4 hours past midnight; marker #3, 6 hours past midnight; and so on.

Now, to determine the correct time:

1. Read the time on the clock in the sky.

2. Subtract 2 hours for every month past March 1. So, for example, if it's May 1, you'd subtract 4 hours.

3. Add 1 hour for daylight saving time.

So in the illustration, for example, it's June 1:

1. The star clock is one-fourth of the way past marker #1, or at about 2:30 A.M.

2. Subtract 2 hours for each month past March 1. Since it's June 1, that's minus 6 hours.

3. Now, add 1 hour for daylight saving time.

Therefore, the time according to the stars on this particular evening is approximately 9:30 P.M.

With practice, your child will eventually be able to tell time by the stars in a matter of seconds. And as he grows up knowing how to read that huge clock in the sky, he'll understand he's not just a victim of time (as many people feel they are), but part of a grand, universal scheme that connects him to all of nature out to the farthest star.

48. How to Find an Owl

A wise old owl sat in an oak.
The more he saw, the less he spoke.
The less he spoke, the more he heard.
Why can't we all be like that bird?

—Edward H. Richards,
a Good Dad of Wise Verse

It's very hard to find an owl. Recluses of the forest, owls have markings that can make them appear two-dimensional and almost invisible. But if you're in the country, you hear that tell-tale *hoootie-hoot,* and your kid's dying to see an owl, you know how to find one.

Here's the secret. Don't look *up* in the air where you'd normally look for birds. Look *down* at the ground under the trees, and keep your eyes peeled for little "pellets" made of grass or hair. Once you've found those, you've found the owl's home. Then you can look up.

At the base of an owl tree, you can tell your kid, she'll always find a number of little balls or "pellets," which are really the leftovers from the owl's latest meals. Owls eat field mice, ground squirrels, birds, even other owls. But they have rather primitive digestive systems. So those parts they can't digest wind up in these pellets. Your kid shouldn't touch the pellets with her hands because they might carry disease. But in a creepy sort of way, they're very interesting to observe.

Once your child finds an owl tree by day, she can return by night and shine a flashlight up into the branches. For some reason, owls don't seem to mind flashlights. So she might be able to catch one at home.

Another great way to find an owl during the day is to watch for crows. Crows hate owls with a passion and chase them mercilessly. A crow will even get together with a whole bunch of his buddies and mob an owl until the bigger bird flees. Songbirds and even hummingbirds will also do this. If your child sees a whole flock of smaller birds squawking alarm calls and swirling after a larger bird, she can bet they've cornered an owl.

A natural loner, the owl loves being evasive and noncommittal. But his sloppy living habits give him away. Clean up your room, kids.

49. How to Mount a Horse

Always know what the other guy expects—then work from there.
—A Good Dad Adage

A kid thinks big, powerful horses should do his bidding. Feeding and brushing them should be enough to make horses his friends. But horses have a well-established etiquette that must be respected. A horse expects a kid to behave himself; when he doesn't, the horse might shy or even nip the kid as he mounts.

So teach your child the proper etiquette for mounting a horse. Always mount from the left side. That's what the horse expects.

If your child's too short to reach the stirrup by himself, lead the horse next to a fence or a truck bed, anything stable that will raise the kid up in the air. The horse's left side should be next to the fence or truck. Then have another adult or an older child stand at the horse's head, holding its reins as the kid mounts.

If your child is tall enough to reach the stirrup without help, have him grasp the reins with his left hand while also holding the pommel (front of the saddle). He should keep the "off rein" (the rein on the horse's right side) tight enough so the horse can't move his head around. Then have him catch the cantle (back of the saddle) with his right hand and slip his left foot into the stirrup. His foot should be far enough into the stirrup to support his weight, but not so far that he can't remove his foot if the horse should suddenly shy.

Then, using his left leg and both arms, have him lift himself quickly but smoothly onto his horse, swinging his right leg over the horse's back. Once he's mounted, have him put his right foot in the right stirrup, and he's ready to ride.

By learning to mount a horse correctly, your child will have learned that even an animal deserves courtesy and respect. And from this early lesson, he may come to realize later in life that whatever his problems with others—spouse, boss, or coworker—common courtesy on his part can help make the relationship work.

50. How to Identify Five Icky Things under a Rock

Not everything that creeps is creepy—or maybe it is.
—A Good Dad Observation

There's a dark side to your kid. Beneath that chipper, charming personality, under all those smiles and jokes, somewhere in a shadowy corner of his otherwise sunny mind, there lurks a longing for crawling things. He finds a dank cellar endlessly fascinating and loves it when he gets gooseflesh. So take him on a tour he'll never forget. Teach him what's hiding under the rocks in your backyard.

Luckily, you know the foremost rule for identifying the most common icky things under a rock: count their legs.

If it looks like a caterpillar or other insect larvae—but has sixty or more legs (two legs on every segment of its body)—it's really a **millipede** (figure a). Caterpillars never have this many legs. *Milli* means "one thousand." But the millipede doesn't really have a thousand legs. Just lots of them.

If it's black, has fourteen legs, looks like a miniature armadillo, and rolls up in a little ball when touched, it's a **pillbug** or **rolypoly** (figure b). If it doesn't roll up, it's a sowbug, also known as a bibble bug, tiggy hog, or wood lice. Like a kangaroo or an opossum mother, a pillbug mom carries her

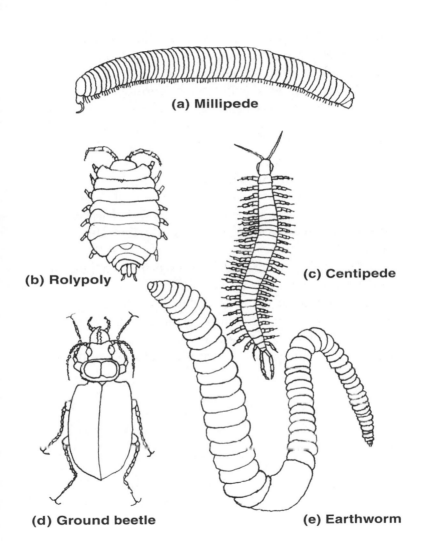

(a) Millipede

(b) Rolypoly

(c) Centipede

(d) Ground beetle

(e) Earthworm

babies around in a pouch. Caution your child not to leave a pillbug in the sun without water; if it dries out too much, it will die. He wouldn't want *that* haunting him.

A close relative to the millipede, the **centipede** (figure c) has about thirty legs, maybe more. If you have a creature with lots of legs and aren't sure which it is, watch how it moves. A millipede sort of glides slowly over the ground like a wave; a centipede tends to wriggle fast—more like a worm. If it flies away on leathered wings, call an exorcist.

A bug with six legs could be any insect. But if it's under a rock and is black or iridescent with a hard shell, chances are it's a **ground beetle** (figure d), a predator who eats other icky things under a rock.

If it has no legs, it's probably just a **worm**. What kind? If it has segments, it's an ordinary **earthworm** (figure e).

Teach your kid these things, and he'll see all those slithering, crawling creatures differently. He might even lose some of his fascination for under-rock-dark-hole dwellers. How can you be scared of anything if you know its name?—unless, of course, it's *Beelzebub*.

51. How to Climb a Ladder

A man's reach should exceed his grasp, else what's a ladder for?
                                                    —A Good Dad Saying

At some point in their young lives, children suddenly become aware of the third dimension. They've been going along quite content with two dimensions: left, right, ahead, and back were enough. Then one day they look and see—*up*. Hey! Up! Why can't I do that direction? They become climbers and never get over *up*. Eventually, your child will discover the ladder, and you can only give her some safe rules to climb by, secrets, if you will, worked out through years of experience by other people who never got over *up*.

One of these secrets is age. A child may be old enough to climb a ladder at around age twelve or so. But that's your decision. Certainly, she should be old enough to remember and apply these six cardinal rules:

1. Never let a ladder contact an electric wire. Metal ones will conduct electricity and so will wooden ones when wet. Stay away from electric wires.

2. The ladder must be in good shape. Make sure no part on it is bent, damaged, or broken.

3. Make sure the base is secure, not on ice, snow, or sand. It should also be one-fourth of the ladder's working height out from the wall, or three feet, whichever is greater.

4. When using an extension ladder, put the ladder in place first and then extend it. Never extend it and then put it in place. Extend while you're on the ground, not while you're on the ladder or roof. Extend it so that the ladder top is three feet above the roofline. Also maintain a three-foot overlap between the extension sections.

5. Always have a second person hold the ladder.

6. Face the ladder at all times when on it. Keep your body centered between the support rails of the ladder. Grip the ladder firmly and never take one hand or foot off a rung until the next hand or foot is firmly engaged.

Like any tool, a ladder helps us do more than we could without it. Since we're going beyond our normal abilities, and maybe even into danger, it's always wise to use tools with caution, but never with fear. Showing a child how to use a ladder correctly is showing her how to safely go where she has never gone before.

DAD FACT

How far is up? About 80,000 feet. After that, it becomes out.

52. How to Attract a Deer
(So You Can Hide and Watch It)

Remember the deer, and never lose what Einstein called your "holy curiosity."

—A Good Dad Motto

Any kid who ever watched *Bambi* gets excited about seeing a wild deer. But getting a close look at a deer in the woods is like trying to trap a moonbeam. Just let a kid spot a deer, and the velvety creature vanishes into the shadows—unless you know a secret that will coax the deer closer so your child can watch.

The secret is this: like children, deer are naturally quite curious. A deer will bolt when he sees a man or a Jeep because he knows those mean danger. But if you appeal to the deer's curiosity, he won't run. Puzzled and intrigued, he'll come closer.

This strategy, called *tolling* a deer, is a technique wildlife photographers often use to get those sensational shots on calendars or in magazines like *National Geographic*. First, of course, you and your child have to be in an area like a national park or natural woodlands where lots of deer live. Go out at dawn or dusk, when deer are most likely to graze. Try to spot a deer in the distance. Once you do, don't show yourselves. Take a white rag and tie it to a bush, letting it flutter in the wind. Then crouch down behind a bush or a rock and wait. With luck, the deer will see your "flag," become curious, and approach to see what it is. Stay hidden, and you'll be surprised how close the deer may come.

If you don't have a white rag, use anything that looks unusual. It's the curiosity factor that counts. This technique will also work very well on antelope, caribou, or wild pigs.

This can be a great adventure for your kid because she doesn't have to hunt for the deer, the deer hunts her. But this special experience should also teach your child something about her own curiosity. The deer is approaching danger but doesn't know it. You could be a hunter. In fact, this technique was developed by hunters. Curiosity should always be coupled with good judgment.

DAD TIP

How to Call a Deer

Every kid knows how to whistle for a dog or call the cat to dinner. But how do you call a deer? Well, naturalists have a secret: clash two deer antlers together. This sounds like two bucks fighting over a doe. Other deer will come to see what the ruckus is about. If you want to try this technique and can find the antlers, it works best during mating season. Just keep a safe distance, because at this time of year, even Bambi can be unpredictable.

53. How to Make a Curve Ball Curve

A curve ball is just a fast ball with an attitude.

—A Good Dad Saying

Myth has it that kids should never throw a curve ball because it will damage their pitching arms. And that's true if they try throwing a curve the way big leaguers do.

But there is a way to make a ball curve that's perfect for a kid's small hand—and won't hurt his arm. The secret is to have your kid tuck his thumb under the ball and then flip his thumb as he throws, much as he'd flip a coin.

This quick flip gives the ball that extra spin it needs to make it curve. Yet because it's thrown with the same arm motion used for a fast ball, this pitch puts no more strain on a kid's arm than an ordinary fast ball does.

But it is important to use the right grip. So have your kid grip the ball with the seams. His index and middle fingers should rest on the ball, so that each finger is just to the left of a seam (figure a). Now have him curl his thumb under the ball, so it rests against the seam on the underside.

Next, as he throws with a normal overhanded motion, have him snap his wrist, so his forefinger and index finger impart spin on the ball. Then as he lets go of the ball—this is

Fingers on "top" of seams

Thumb tucked "under" bottom seam

(a)

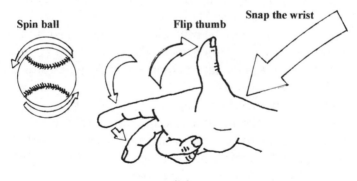

Spin ball

Flip thumb

Snap the wrist

(b)

the trick—have him flip his thumb to give the ball extra spin (figure b).

With practice, he'll be able to make that high hard one break in over home plate like a darting hornet. And then he'll come to realize fully the value of his own actions. Whether or not the ball curves, depends on what he did to it before it left his hand. It's just him and the baseball. Nothing else counts.

DAD FACT

Does the Curve Ball Really Curve?

For many years, some folks insisted it didn't, that the apparent curve was just an optical illusion. But pitchers kept throwing curves. One even quipped, "Maybe the curve ball doesn't curve. But if you hide from me behind a tree 60½ feet away (the distance from the pitcher's mound to home plate), I'll beat you up with a baseball." Finally, scientists entered the spirited debate and proved forever that, yes, the curve ball does curve. According to one calculation, the most a ball can curve is 17½ inches. Since home plate is 17 inches wide, this means a perfect curve can start on the inside corner and pass over home plate ½ inch outside the strike zone.

54. How to Shoot a Free Throw

Big shots are only little shots who keep shooting.

—Christopher Morley,
a Good Dad of Light Essays and Novels

When kids start shooting free throws for the first time, they unconsciously make umpteen adjustments at once. Paying attention only to what's happening at the hoop, they move around like crazy at the free throw line, angling their bodies this way and that, dancing forward and back as if they were learning to minuet. They become lousy shooters.

But you know a secret that will help your kid greatly increase his odds of success: make sure he shoots the same way every time.

A free throw is deceptive; it looks as if it's always the same shot. But, in fact, there are many subtle variations. How your kid holds the ball, where he places his hands, the way he touches the ball, the angle of his body when he shoots, how he launches the ball toward the basket—all these and a myriad of other variables will affect his chance of putting the ball the same place every time: through the hoop. By noting all these variations and seeing clearly what works and what doesn't, he'll become more consistently accurate.

So have him try this:

1. Count the number of steps from the edge to the center of the free throw circle. Then stand there. Tell him to stand with both toes on the line. This way, he's squarely facing the basket.

2. Pick out some spot on the basketball—perhaps on the lines of the ball—where he can put the fingertips of his shooting hand every time. Have him choose another spot for his nonshooting hand.

3. Now have him lift the ball squarely above his head, using the same position every time, and loft it toward the basket. He should try to make the ball come off the same fingers every time and avoid letting his palms touch the ball.

After trying several shots and seeing where the ball goes, he can then adjust his shooting. One small step at a time. He'll develop "a touch." And as he learns to shoot, he'll also learn success is a craft, and those who succeed often simply know secrets less successful folks don't.

55. How to See the Big Picture

People's minds are only as small—or big—as the things they think about.

—A Good Dad Axiom

Much of a kid's life is spent focusing on small details. Whether she's trying to master long division or to spell *antidisestablishmentarianism*, little details *do* count. And she should pay attention. But there are days in any kid's life when she needs to step back and take a bigger view of a problem or situation. Maybe she has a major science report due in a week, and she's so bogged down in the niggling details she can't get started.

Fortunately, you know the secret that will take her mind off those minor worries so she can see the big picture: teach her how big the universe is.

No kid can ponder the size of the universe without asking big questions. So wait until dark. Then take her out under the stars. Tell her about something so big she can hardly imagine it and so old she can barely believe it.

Just start talking casually about the stars. Tell her the stars look very close together up there in the sky. But, actually, they're so far apart that if our sun were shrunk to the size of the period at the end of this sentence, the closest star to us (called Alpha Centauri) would be a period in a book thirty miles away. And for stars, that's a close distance.

Tell her the stars often look as if they're only an arm's length away. But, in fact, they're so far away that the light from them takes many years to reach us, even though light travels incredibly fast (about 186,000 miles a second). The light from most of the stars she sees tonight started traveling toward the Earth before she was born. Some of the light striking her eyes tonight is so ancient it started on its journey toward Earth before Columbus discovered America. Even before Julius Caesar was emperor of Rome. Or before dinosaurs walked the Earth.

Let her ponder this a while. Then tell her that some of those stars we see only as pinpoints of light are unbelievably bright and heavy. One star up there is 15,150 times brighter than the sun. Another is 208,000 times brighter. Some stars are so heavy that just one tiny teaspoon of their star matter would weigh more than the family car, even more than the Empire State Building. Some have such strong gravity that even light can't escape from them. So they become black holes. Throw in every gee-whiz astronomy fact you can find.

As your child ponders the awesome mysteries of the stars, she'll come to wonder why she ever got bogged down in that science report. It will suddenly seem a lot smaller than it did this afternoon. And later in life, she'll come to be known as a person of vision who doesn't get stopped by minor details, because she knows how to see the big picture.

56. How to Break In a Baseball Glove

Well begun is half done.

—Aristotle, the Good Dad of Western Thought

You've bought your child a genuine leather baseball glove, a real beauty. But unless it's broken in properly, a new glove can actually make your kid play *worse*. Why? Because a new glove is so stiff it can cause her to drop a crucial line drive or fumble away a hot grounder.

So here's how to help your kid break in her new glove so she can make amazing "look what I have here" catches that have eyes popping all over the park:

1. Before she begins, have her bury her face in the glove and smell that sweet leather. Never for the rest of her life will she forget that delicious smell.

2. Have her sprinkle a few drops of neat's-foot oil into the pocket and work them into the leather.

3. Now have her put on the glove and pound a deep pocket into it with her free fist. This may take a dozen or more blows.

4. Place a ball (the kind she'll be catching) in the pocket and fold the fingers and thumb of the glove over the ball (figure a).

5. Wrap three or four big, fat rubber bands tightly around the whole glove (figure b).

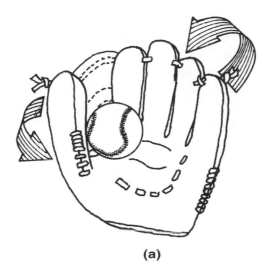

(a)

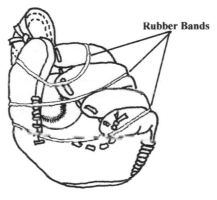

Rubber Bands

(b)

6. Leave the glove clamped like this around the ball all night.

7. Repeat steps 1-5 every night for a week or more. Some pros reportedly take two weeks to break in a glove.

During the break-in period, remind your child to work a few drops of neat's–foot oil into the pocket before each day's use. Whenever she's standing in the field waiting for a ball, encourage her to pound her fist hard into the pocket to keep molding it.

Finally, when storing the glove for the winter, once again have her rub the pocket with oil, place the ball in the pocket, and wrap the rubber bands around it. Come spring, your child will have a glove that will gobble up ground balls and snag flies out of the sky. She will also have learned that advantages are not always gifts, but can be earned with conscientious effort.

DAD FACT

Is It a Mitt or a Glove?

Baseball novices often use the words "glove" and "mitt" interchangeably. But a glove has separate fingers; a mitt doesn't. So when you're talking baseball, just remember this. A catcher has a **mitt**. A first baseman can have either a **mitt** or a **glove**. An infielder or an outfielder has a **glove**.

---

57. How to Find a Needle in a Haystack

Somebody said it couldn't be done.
But he with a chuckle replied
That "maybe it couldn't," but he would be one
Who wouldn't say so till he'd tried.
      —Edgar A. Guest, a Good Dad of Humorous Verse

Some people seem to make careers out of telling others, "It can't be done." No matter what a kid's dreams, as he goes through life, he's bound to run into a few of these wet blankets. "Never expect much, and you won't be disappointed," they warn. Or, to cite an old adage, "That's as impossible as finding a needle in a haystack."

Fortunately, as a good dad, you know a practical way to impress on your kid forever the idea that nothing's impossible. You just happen to know how to find that proverbial haystack needle: use a magnet.

To drive this message home so your kid will never forget it, you might want to use a little dad showmanship. Wait for one of those inevitable times when your kid says, "I can't." It matters little what he imagines he "can't" do—whether it's hit a basketball hoop or learn math. You reply, "*Can't?* Are you kidding me? You can do anything. Why, I'll bet you even could find a needle in a haystack." When he protests, show him how.

These days, of course, haystacks are harder to come by than they were when more people lived in Kansas. But a big pile of cut grass or dry autumn leaves will work just as well. Simply bury one or more ordinary needles in the "haystack." Then give your kid a large horseshoe magnet to burrow through the "hay." In a matter of seconds—or with a larger haystack, maybe minutes—he'll emerge with the needle and a grin on his face as broad as a jack-o'-lantern's.

And years later, whenever he's told he "can't" accomplish his dreams, he'll only smile and reply, "I'll bet you're one of those people who also think it's impossible to find a needle in a haystack."

58. How to Cast with a Fly Rod

Talent without practice is like a bucket with a hole in it.
—A Good Dad Saying

It takes many patient hours to become proficient with a fly rod. In fact, it's been said that no child ever went fly fishing, because it takes so many years to learn about the equipment and how to cast that by the time you learn it all, you're no longer a child. So when a kid's first efforts at fly casting produce a line so tangled it looks like a bird's nest, he can easily get discouraged—and quit.

You can solve this problem with a little colored yarn. Have your child practice casting with a wooden dowel onto which you've tied a five-foot length of brightly colored rug yarn. He can then watch and easily see how the line behaves as he whips it back and forth.

The important thing while fly casting is to get a nice, tight, U-shaped bend in the line on both the backward and forward parts of the cast. With brightly colored yarn, he can see this U- shape a lot easier. The yarn acts like those "streamers" football cheerleaders use. As long as it's whipped back and forth, it hangs in the air. But it's important for him to whip it smoothly.

Once he achieves a nice, tight, U-shaped bend in the yarn on both the backward and forward parts of his cast, he can then move on to a real line. The trick here is for him to play out more and more line with each cast, a little at a time. Have him pull about twenty feet of line from the reel with his left hand (if he's right-handed) and hold the line lightly. It should run easily through his fingers as he does a series of "false casts." Make sure he still has those tight U-shaped bends. At first, let him cast into the distance just to see how the rod feels as he lets out more line.

He may want to practice like this for, say, thirty minutes a day for as long as it takes. But once you see he's ready, you can then add a target like a garbage can lid or a hula hoop. After several false casts, have him snap the rod forward, this time aiming at the target. He should let the fly land gently on the target, as any self-respecting insect would on water. When your kid gets the hang of all this, increase the challenge by tucking the target under a shrub or low-hanging tree.

Fly fishing teaches and rewards patience, and out on the tranquil, slow-moving river, patience comes easily. Even if he grows up to a hectic, stress-filled life, lacking in all the harmony he's now learning to enjoy, he'll still have a place to go where he can find some of the peace you've taught him. Patience is never really lost, not when you have a place like a fly-fishing river for safekeeping.

59. How to Bait Cast

If people concentrated on the really important things in life, there'd be a shortage of fishing poles.
        —Doug Larson, a Good Dad of Many Pithy Quips

Most kids love fishing. Maybe it's the early morning outing with you through the woods when the whole world seems fresh and new. Or maybe it's just having a good excuse to go wading. But once they try to cast, they usually bungle the job because their hands aren't big or strong enough to handle a rod and reel together.

Fortunately, you know about a reel that's so simple even an eight- or nine-year-old can learn to cast by herself. It's the push-button reel. The line is completely housed in a casing and fed out through a single opening at the front. On the back of the casing, there's a push button large and easy enough for a child's thumb to manage. This one button does it all.

When your child's ready to fish, have her stand facing the direction she means to cast. Her right foot (if she's right-handed) should be slightly forward. Now have her push down on the button and hold it. The lure at the end of her rod will drop a short distance, then stop. She's ready to cast.

Have her concentrate on the spot she's aiming for and point the rod at that spot. She should draw the rod tip smoothly back to the two o'clock position. Then, without stopping, she should snap the rod toward the target. At the eleven o'clock position, she should raise her thumb and release the button. The line will feed out smoothly.

To make sure she hits her target, she can do one of two things: (1) depress the button again, which will brake the line and cause the lure to drop, or (2) "feather" the line, by letting it run out between her left thumb and index finger (if she's right-handed). The first method is the easiest for a small child. The second method's trickier, but with practice, your daughter will learn to slow the line and bring it to a stop exactly on target.

To reel the line back in, she merely cranks the lever around. But she shouldn't try reeling in her line when the button is depressed; that's when there's a brake on the cranking lever. To a child, a rod and reel are clearly adult tools. It matters little that they've been made push-button simple. Learning how to bait cast will make her feel wonderfully accomplished. And even if she doesn't catch a fish, she'll catch a beautiful morning.

60. How to Make a (Better) Paper Airplane

The happiest person is the one who makes his dreams fly.
—A Good Dad Maxim

Paper airplanes are a dad's nemesis. That's because our kids somehow expect our planes to fly farther and better than the ones they fold. Usually they don't. They swoop to the left and plunge at our feet. No more. Now there's a paper airplane that flies like a good dad plane should. It won't stall, and if this plane cannot make it across your living room, you probably live in a mansion.

This plane does require some tinkering. Your kid has to be especially careful to open the slots under each wing exactly the same amount (about one-eighth of an inch or less for best effect). But when he gets it going—beautiful!

1. He should fold one end of a regular sheet of paper back on itself about one-fourth the length of the paper (figure a).

2. Now he should turn over the paper and fold it in half down the middle (figure b).

3. Next he should fold point 1 down below the center crease as shown (figure c).

4. Then he should fold point 2 down below the center crease on the other side so it coincides with point 1. He should then tape points 1 and 2 together, running the tape under the airplane (figure d).

5. Next have him fold wing A down as shown (figure e) and then fold down wing B on the other side so it coincides with wing A (figure f).

6. Now he should raise both wings and tape them at two points as shown (figure g). Then he should make cut X (figure h) and push the tail up through the fuselage.

7. Next he should fold the wings down as in step 5 and cut them to shape, as indicated by dotted line C-D (figure i).

8. Now he should raise the wings.

9. Then have him insert a small paper clip in the nose. The whole clip should be inside the nose, so you can't even see it from the outside.

10. Finally, he should pull out the slots under the wings as shown (figure j), creating about one-eighth inch between the top and bottom of each wing. He should make sure the slots are open an equal amount. And presto! He's ready to try his first flight.

Paper airplanes—even great ones like this one—require many small adjustments. After one or two flights, they usually demand repair to the nose, the wings and, in this case, the slots. If the plane doesn't sail clear across the living room on the first try, do some delicate fine-tuning by folding the wings upward in a dihedral (a slightly upward V-shape).

As you and your kid are fine-tuning your planes and getting ready to strafe the living room again, it's a good time to teach him the importance of paying attention to details.

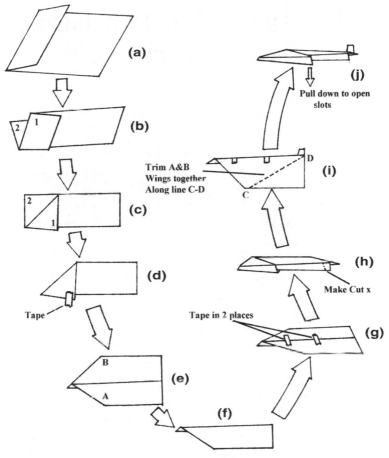

(a)

(b)

(c)

Tape

(d)

B

A

(e)

(f)

Wings A & B folded down together

Tape in 2 places

(g)

Make Cut x

(h)

Trim A&B
Wings together
Along line C-D

C

D

(i)

Pull down to open
slots

(j)

61. How to Build Confidence on the Baseball Field

If you can dream it, you can do it.
—Walt Disney, the Good Dad of Mickey Mouse

You know your child plays baseball well. You've hit flies to him and watched him make quiet, competent plays. But when he's standing on the field during a game, his talents abandon him like passengers from a sinking ship. And sink he does, as he staggers under an easy pop fly or lets a one-hopper get past him. Plainly, your kid's lost his confidence.

Just as plainly, you can help him find it again. The next time he's on the field, just have him silently repeat seven short words: "I hope the ball comes to me."

Then tell him to vividly visualize what he'll do when the ball does come to him. Let's imagine there are runners on first and third. An easy fly ball comes his way. He catches it. But now does he throw it to first, or try to nail the runner at home? What if it's a long fly he has to catch on the run? Does he still throw home? Or does he fake a throw home and try to nail the runner at second? Or, suppose it's a clean base hit? If the batter is loafing on his way to first, could your kid make a surprise throw and get him out? When major league players pull off this last coup, the park goes suddenly silent. Amazing! The runner's out! A few minutes later, the crowd's still agog with disbelief. That fielder threw out a runner on a solid base hit!

As your kid stands on his field of dreams, rehearsing all the possibilities, an interesting thing happens; instead of worrying about how he'll perform and fretting he might screw up, he becomes so deeply focused on the game he no longer even thinks about failing. He's too busy mentally preparing himself for success.

So if that guy on first thinks he can easily take second on the next fly hit to your kid, he's in for a rude surprise. And when your kid's grown, he'll know that the journey to excellence always begins with a vision. If asked by a supervisor to prepare a report, he won't groan, "Oh, my God! A report?" He'll already have imagined what he'd do if that report came to him.

62. How to Pick Out a Good Kitten

Your kitten's job, I solemnly bet,
Is to become the cat you've never met.

—A Good Dad Observation

To kids, all kittens look equally adorable. So when it's time to pick out a pet, they'll choose a kitten for all the wrong reasons. "Look at that black one with the white feet: we could call him Mittens!" Or, "This gray one pounced fastest on the yarn. He really likes me."

Yet you know a cute, cuddly little kitten can eventually become an obnoxious, irritating cat who claws the drapes and always misbehaves. So prevent disaster before it strikes. Teach your child how to pick out the right kitten. The secret is understanding that the kitten's personality won't change. However the feline behaves as a baby will be the way it also acts as an adult.

Your kid doesn't want the first kitten that runs to her. It'll be too aggressive when it grows up, the sort of cat that demands attention, scratches the sofa, and never behaves. But she doesn't want a cat that's too timid, either. If a kitten withdraws from being picked up or meows when it's handled, it could be aloof and unfriendly as an adult. Also see how the kitten plays with its brothers and sisters. If it's too aggressive, it may be irritating when it's older.

Have her carry the kitten into another room, away from its mother, set it down by itself, and see how it reacts. Does it crouch, miserable and afraid? Or is it alert and curious? Now have her make some loud noise, such as clapping her hands together above the kitten's head, to see how it reacts. Does it look alertly around to see where the noise came from, then calmly proceed with its business? Or does it try to hide and meow for its mother?

Finally, ask the owners about the kitten's handling history. If it's been handled at least twenty minutes a day, it will probably be smarter. If it's seldom petted but it's still under eight weeks old, ask the owners if your child can come by once every day or so to handle and talk to the kitten. A kitten that's regularly talked to will become a friendlier cat.

The kitten that passes all these tests with flying colors will become a cat your whole family can love. And your kid will have learned she can learn to read others—cats or people—just by watching how they behave.

63. How to Identify a Meteorite

Star light, star bright, first star I see tonight.
I wish I may, I wish I might, find myself a meteorite.
—A Good Dad Poem for Meteorite Hunters

Most kids are mesmerized by falling stars. Imagine! That other-worldly light streaking across the sky could have come from another planet, even a star in some distant galaxy. But that's where the fantasy ends, because most kids think meteors burn up in the atmosphere. So picture your kid's surprise when you tell him that everywhere on the Earth, there may be as many as ten meteorites per square mile. Chances are, he'll look at you as if you've just told him you know where Blackbeard's lost treasure is hidden.

The secret to identifying meteorites is that they all contain a good percentage of iron. This means your kid can tell a meteorite by three important identifiable characteristics: (1) it is distinctively heavier than a rock of the same size; (2) it is black on the outside because, as it passes through the Earth's atmosphere, the iron burns, giving the meteorite a black patina; and (3) it responds to a magnet. So if your kid ever finds a rock that's amazingly heavy, shiny black, and magnetic, he's probably got himself a meteorite, maybe the one he saw tonight.

One final test. Another rock, magnetite, is also heavy, black, and magnetic. But it leaves a black streak when rubbed against a harder surface, like an unglazed porcelain tile. A meteorite doesn't.

You can add that meteorites fall everywhere, but he's most apt to find one in places they've already been found. One place is Antarctica (not particularly handy). But other good meteorite-hunting grounds include dry lake beds, desert areas where rocks have been sorted from sand by the wind, and rocky moraines left behind by glaciers.

A kid who looks for meteorites is a practical dreamer, the kind who grows up to design huge dams and send astronauts into space. But a kid who finds a meteorite is a *lucky* practical dreamer, and there's no limit to what he might accomplish.

DAD FACT

Is It a Meteoroid, a Meteor, or a Meteorite?

A rock that's still in space is a **meteoroid**. A rock falling through the atmosphere and burning is a **meteor**. The rock you find on the ground is a **meteorite**.

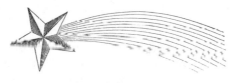

64. How to Use a Hammer

The building of a thousand houses begins with a single nail.
—A Good Dad Proverb

Learning to use a hammer is a lot like becoming a superhero. *POW!* With the strength of Hercules. *WHAM!* With a fist of steel (really). *SOCKO!* For Truth and Justice.

The only difference is that superheroes are playthings of a child's imagination, while a hammer is a real tool that has lifted mankind to a super-being level. To use a hammer correctly, your child only has to learn two simple skills:

The correct grip: Using figure a, show your child how to hold the hammer by gripping it at the end. When the hammer is held correctly, two imaginary lines (A and B) should be parallel to each other.

The correct swing: The secret here lies in bending the elbow and wrist without moving the shoulder. Using figure b, show your child how to flex his wrist up as he lifts his arm at the elbow and how to flex his wrist down as he swings down. Up-down. Bending elbow and flexing wrist.

Once your child has mastered these two skills, have him hold a nail upright and start it into the wood by giving it a few light taps with the hammer. For just this few seconds, he'll want to hold his elbow steady and move only his wrist.

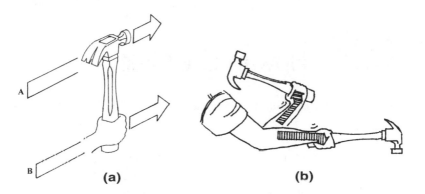

(a)   **(b)**

Once the nail is started, make sure he moves his free hand out of the line of fire (very important!). Then have him drive the nail with firm, heavy blows, using the motion he learned in figure b.

If the nail goes smooth and straight into the wood, he's "working smart." If it suddenly bends or cants over, he's not. With practice, he'll soon become a master. It's the next best thing to giving him the power of *SHAZAM*.

DAD SAFETY TIP

The impact of a hammer on a nail is loud enough to damage hearing and powerful enough to make flakes of steel fly suddenly off the hammer like darts. So have your child wear earplugs and safety goggles while hammering. Most tool manufacturers use good steel. But still, flaws can creep in. So before using a hammer, examine it closely. If it is already chipped, it could chip again. Discard it and choose another one.

65. How to Use Glue

Too much of a good thing can be a bad thing.

—A Good Dad Adage

When children use glue, they seem to believe the more the better. They apparently think that if a little glue holds two pieces of wood or plastic together, a lot forms an unbreakable bond. Slathering on the stuff, they wind up with a seam so dripping with hardened glue that it looks like a candy house covered with frosting. Yet too much glue makes a joint brittle, so it's more apt to break.

So teach your kid how to use glue. The secret: be temperate; don't just slop it on.

Have your kid take two pieces of wood or plastic that need repair. First have her read the instructions on the glue bottle or tube to see how long it takes to set. Then have her clean the surfaces of the two pieces she's repairing. Dirt will keep glue out of the pores and weaken the adhesive bond.

Now have her spread the glue—in moderation—on both surfaces and clamp them together. With some superglues, she can just hold the two surfaces together for thirty seconds. With others, she'll need to use a vise or clamp and perhaps even leave the surfaces pressed together overnight. If she clamps two boards together at one end and the wood's not perfectly straight, they can spring apart at the other end. So when gluing two wooden surfaces, she should make sure *all* parts of the wood are clamped firmly together.

Learning to use glue properly teaches your child the value of moderation and self-restraint. Enthusiasm is a virtue in many pursuits. But it's always wise to know when enough is enough.

66. How to Make a Buddy

A buddy is like a friend without the pressure.

—A Good Dad Observation

Your kid has come home from school upset. "I hate that dumb school," he groans. When you probe deeper, he confides that nobody in school "likes" him. Then he asks, "Do you know how I can make a friend?"

"Nope," you reply. "But I know how you can make a buddy." There are no easy rules for making a friend. But, as a good dad knows, there is one clear-cut way to make a buddy: find somebody who likes to do what you like to do, whether it's collecting bugs, studying the stars, or skateboarding. Friends are based on who likes whom (very elusive). Buddies are based on who likes *what*.

Your kid can best find someone who shares his interests by asking lots of kids lots of questions. If your kid is shy, you might want to help him develop a "script" to get him started. Each kid's script will, of course, be unique, depending on his passions. But here's a semi-tongue-in-cheek example for a kid who likes spiders: "Hi, my name's Austin. What's yours? What do you think of arachnids, anyway?" Once he finds a kid who shares his interest, have him toss in a few "gee whiz" facts and queries: "Since a spider web is stronger than a strand of steel the same size, maybe we should make skyscrapers out of spider webs." Or, "Did you know a spider digests his dinner and *then eats it?*" Or, "I've been wondering, why doesn't a spider ever get caught in his own web?"

Help your kid brainstorm some eye-poppers that would work best for him. By being genuinely curious about a topic he loves—whether it's raising hamsters or playing soccer—your kid will soon forget his self-consciousness and start acting happy-go-lucky.

By the end of the school year, your child might have one buddy who talks about nothing but dinosaurs, a second who likes playing checkers, and a third who's crazy about airplanes. By learning how to make a buddy, he'll gain confidence in his ability to relate to people on many levels. And, as some of his buddies slowly turn into deep, lasting friends, he'll come to understand that friendships just evolve naturally when he forgets about himself and cares about others.

67. How to Pick Up a Crab

A person of weak character is like a crab: he'll try to look as if he knows where he's going when he's really just running sideways.
—A Good Dad Saying

To a child, most crabs just look like big bugs with lots of legs. As a result, a kid may grab a crab anywhere—and get a nasty claw locked on her finger. The only way to remove a painful crab claw from a screaming child's hand is to clip the claw deftly off with scissors.

Fortunately, as a good dad knows, you can avoid this scenario by teaching your child to pick up a crab correctly. The secret? It's the key to most success in life: pay attention to the details.

When your child looks closely, she'll see that most crabs have eight little legs at one end of their body and two big "legs" (which are really claws) at the other end. To pick up a crab safely, your child simply has to grab the crab by the shell, *behind* the claws and in front of the eight wriggly legs (see figure).

Stress that it's very important to look closely before you pick up a crab. Why? Because a crab usually walks sideways or backwards. So when the crab's running or walking along the shore, it's all too easy for a child to grab him from the wrong end.

It's also important to pick up a crab by his shell, not his legs. Why? Because nature has equipped the crab with a built-in way to escape. Without hurting himself, he can simply break off his leg and scurry away. Later, he'll grow a new leg (one of the miracles of nature). Once a child has collected a crab, she can keep him in an aquarium for a while to watch him. But, remember, some crabs can't breathe when they're out of water.

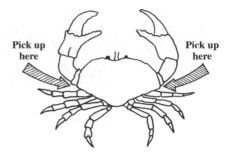

The safest of all ways for a child to pick up a crab is to avoid using her hands and use tongs, instead. The crab is ugly to look at, but has some of the sweetest meat of the sea. Which just goes to show that looks can be deceiving.

DAD FACT

Every year, a mother shore crab lays thousands of tiny eggs, each one much tinier than the period at the end of this sentence.

---

68. How to Multiply Any Number by 11

Always look for a faster way to do the job right.

—A Good Dad Maxim

Any kid past third grade can multiply a number by 10; just add a zero. Multiplying by 11 is also easy—until he goes past 99. But what's 11 times 14? Or 11 times 3,473? At this point, most kids would drag out their trusty calculators. Not yours. Your kid knows how to multiply any number by 11 in a microsecond.

Here's the secret: have him take any number he wants to multiply by 11 and add a zero. Then have him add the number he started with. So 14 times 11 becomes 140 (add the zero) + 14 (the original number), or 154. 17 times 11 is 170 + 17, or 187. And 3,473 times 11 is 34,730 (add the zero) + 3,473 (the original number), which equals 38,203. As a good dad knows, multiplication is just fast addition. With this shortcut, your kid is simply multiplying the number by 10, then again by 1.

With numbers like 3,473, your child will probably need a notepad and pencil. But he can still get the answer faster than most kids can enter the figures on a computer. And he'll have learned that to work smart, he first needs to master the right principles. Then he'll know how to take shortcuts.

How to Multiply Any Number
That Has All Digits Alike

Eleven is a special case of a number that has both digits the same. But larger numbers with all digits alike are still easy to multiply. Simply make the repeating-digit number the multiplier.

Example: 99 × 65

Solution: Make 99 the multiplier. This way you only have to multiply by 9 rather than by 6 and 5.

```
        6 5
     ×  9 9
      5 8 5
    5 8 5
    6,4 3 5
```

With larger numbers the process becomes even faster and easier:

```
        6 5
   ×  9,9 9 9
      5 8 5
    5 8 5
  5 8 5
5 8 5
6 4 9,9 3 5
```

Notice how the 9s show up in the middle of the quotient. So 65 × 999,999 equals 64,999,935 and 65 × 999,999,999,999 equals 64,999,999,999,935. Neat, huh?

69. How to Use a Level

Tools make ordinary people extraordinary.

—A Good Dad Saying

Your kid's decided to hang her favorite posters on the walls of her room. By the time you get home from work, she's been at it for hours. You take one peek in her room and Whoa! The posters are canted at so many different angles her walls look like a nightmarish Picasso creation. "I tried eyeballing them. But that's the best I can do," she protests.

"Um, let me show you how to use a level," you suggest. You know with a level she can get those posters perfectly straight. You also know how to help her use a level correctly: just center the bubble.

Every level, whatever its size or shape, has at least one little tube of colored liquid containing a bubble. Carpenter's levels have three bubble tubes. But many simpler levels have only one. When the level is gently placed against the top of a poster (or picture frame)—and that bubble is exactly in the middle of the tube—the poster will be perfectly parallel to the floor.

Have your kid straighten all her posters horizontally by placing the level along the top of each poster and centering the bubble. Then have her straighten them vertically by placing the level along the side of each poster and centering the bubble.

Tools extend human capabilities. With a tool, we can do a task better or build a structure bigger than we could without this weapon for civilization. Some day, your child will need to use a tool, but there may not be time enough to learn how. So teach her now how to use lots of tools. You'll be helping her make an improved version of herself.

70. How to Paddle a Canoe

Be strong,
We're not here to drift
We have hard work to do
And paddles to lift.

—A Good Dad Poem about Canoeing

When kids have to ride in the backseat, they feel left out and unimportant. No one ever asks their advice, and they can't even see down the road. But in a canoe, suddenly a kid gets to sit up front. At last! She feels as if she's in charge of the family fun.

Happily, you can let your kid relish the thrill of paddling her own canoe and still do it safely because you know a secret; it's the paddler in *back* who controls the boat.

The person in front only has to paddle straight. But she still has to paddle to do her part. So teach your child the skill of paddling a straight canoe. It's simpler than she might think.

1. Start in easy water like a still lake or a smooth stream. Have your kid hold the paddle as straight up as possible (figure a). One hand should be on top of the paddle, the other hand on the throat of the paddle, about six inches above the blade.

2. Now have her reach forward as far as possible. Her upper hand will be far over the gunwale of the canoe (figure a). She'll pull straight back, keeping the path of the blade parallel to the direction the canoe's going (figure b). She should reach forward

(a)

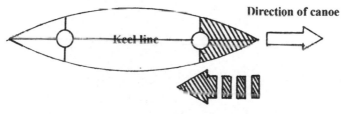

Direction of canoe

Keel line

Direction of stroke

(b)

with her upper hand and pull with the lower hand. Reach, pull. Reach, pull. It's that simple. It's important to paddle cleanly. If she lets the paddle wobble, the canoe will turn. But that's no problem because you're there in the back, quietly ready to adjust.

3. Now practice paddling in unison. Have her paddle on the left, while you paddle on the right. If the canoe begins to head too much toward the right, switch sides.

4. The backstroke—which is really the canoe's "brake"—is the exact opposite of the stroke in step 2. Teach your child to reach as far back as possible with her paddle and push forward while you do the same.

Gradually, as she gets more strokes under her belt, your child will learn how the canoe responds to each turn of the paddle. You'll have remained the unseen hand that makes everything safe while she relishes her moment of "driving." And she'll also have learned that two people can often get ahead faster by pooling their strengths and working together.

71. How to Choose Properties to Buy in Monopoly

There are three reasons to buy properties in Monopoly: location, location, location.

—A Good Dad Saying

Monopoly is one of those "fun family games" that frequently wind up in tantrums and tears. Losing is frustrating, no matter how earnestly parents try to teach kids to "lose well." Fortunately, you needn't make your kid a good loser. You know a secret that will help him *win*.

As he goes through life, your kid will often hear that someone who invests in the right real estate or the right stocks was just "lucky." Not true. Luck may play a role. But a winner also knows secrets others don't know. So what secret will help your kid win at Monopoly? Buy the orange ones—New York, St. James, and Tennessee.

Why? Because those are the properties players land on most often. They also offer the best return on his money. Some people have actually gone to great extent to figure this out mathematically. While the orange properties (and to a lesser extent, the maroons and light blues) are the best investments, the utilities and the green properties are the worst. What's wrong with the greens? They cost too much to buy and develop. By the time a kid has built a few houses on the greens, he's out of money. Then the minute he lands on any space—even a railroad—he's bankrupt. Occasionally, some player will build hotels on the greens and manage to wipe everyone out. But have your kid watch several games closely. He'll see the mogul who builds hotels on orange—especially early in the game—almost always wins.

Once your kid gets old enough to understand "percentage of profit," you can explain this even more clearly. Basically, the higher the POP, the better the deal. On the light blues, the POP is 53 percent. On the oranges, the POP is less—46.9 percent—but players land on them more often. What's the POP on the reds, yellows, and greens with hotels? Less than 40 percent. Paltry. Trade those off.

Once your kid learns a few Monopoly tricks, you'll have fewer tantrums (at least from *him*), and he'll have learned a key lesson: in Monopoly, as in life, it's good to be lucky, but it's even better to know what you're doing.

72. How to Tell How Tall a Tree Is

"Mathematics is the language with which God has written the universe."
—Galileo, the Good Dad of Astronomy

Kids are constantly curious. Why aren't frogs blue? Why can't I smell the inside of my nose? How tall is that tree? You may be stumped by that nose query, but you know some frogs *are* blue. And you can answer that third question in a snap.

You know *exactly* how to tell how tall a tree is because you know a secret leftover from your high school geometry class: similar triangles are . . . well, *similar*. And this means that if your kid uses a stick to create a triangle that's similar to the tree, he can immediately tell how tall it is.

Here's how:

1. Have him find a straight stick longer than his arm. If nothing else is available, a broom handle will do.

2. Have him extend his arm out perfectly straight. Then lay the stick along his arm. Now have him grasp the stick so the part above his grip is exactly the length of his arm.

3. As he holds the stick straight out from his body, have him look along the stick at the tree. Have him "eyeball" the tree, lining up the top of the stick exactly with the top of the tree and the bottom of the stick exactly with the bottom of the tree trunk (see figure). He should not move his hand nor his eyes to do this. Instead, have him walk toward or away from the tree until the stick above his grip is perfectly aligned with it.

4. Now have him look at the ground. Guess what? The distance between him and the tree is also exactly how tall the tree is.

Tell him he's just had his first geometry lesson. Years later, when his pals are sweating advanced math in high school, he'll remember the tree and the stick and think: "Geometry? No problem. My dad started teaching me that when I was six."

73. How to Dribble a Basketball

Never despair. Success may be right at your fingertips.
—A Good Dad Adage

Your kid's short, and basketball seems made for the tall kids. Yet you know one part of the game where the little players shine. That's in the dribble.

And the secret to good dribbling is in the fingertips. Once your child learns to use her fingertips (not her palms) to control the ball, she can start faster, change directions more confidently, and run harder from one end of the court to the other.

She'll soon learn her fingertips act like spongy little shock absorbers, stopping the ball quickly at the top of its bounce. Then they return a springy, bouncy energy to the ball as she pushes it back to the floor. There's control in those marvelous little digits.

Once her fingertips develop a "feel" for the ball, have her dribble standing still—but blindfolded. Kids who can dribble without watching the ball are terrors on the court. They can quickly spot an open teammate and know the positions of all the defenders.

As her ball handling improves, your child will learn it's not just size that counts. In basketball, as in life, everyone has something valuable to contribute.

A Great Dribbling Drill

This drill will help your kid improve her dribbling skills.
First, set up obstacles (like empty cardboard boxes or milk
cartons) in the driveway. Let your child practice dribbling
figure eights around all this stuff. Have her practice keeping
her non-dribbling hand up for balance. Also, as she weaves
her way around these obstacles, have her switch hands,
handling the ball first with her right hand, then her left.
Have her start slow for accuracy, then work on building up
speed until she can do everything on the run.

74. How to Rescue a Baby Bird

Let us permit nature to have her way; she understands her business better than we do.

—Montaigne, a Good Dad of the French Essay

With his scraggly baby feathers and feeble attempts to fly, an orphan bird is a sorry sight. Then there are his pathetic cries for mercy. "Help me! Help me! Come on, guys, a little pity on us birds!" he seems to cheep. And, of course, your child's gentle heart goes out to the poor creature. What can she do?

Fortunately, you know exactly how she can best help the bird: leave it alone. If he's in any danger, she can put him on a nearby perch, out of harm's way. But she should not carry him away. If she does, she's truly made him an orphan.

In the first place, the baby bird's cries for help are not for human ears. Those plaintive sounds he makes are just for his mom. He wants only her help, no one else's. And his mother is probably hiding nearby, watching and waiting for you and your child to leave so she *can* help.

Once you're out of the way, the mother bird will find the little fellow and feed him. She may even get him back in the nest. How? By carrying him home. Birds have been observed in the wild carrying their babies in many different ways. Some pick

177

the baby bird up by the head. Others carry him between their legs or under their wings. A few baby birds have even been seen riding on their mother's or father's back.

So tell your child to leave the bird alone even if he's been injured. And if someone else has already "rescued" the bird, she should urge them to return the baby to the place they found him. It's illegal to keep almost any wild bird captive. But if your child thinks the bird really needs help, she can notify a licensed caregiver by contacting the Audubon Society, game department, or the Society for the Prevention of Cruelty to Animals (SPCA).

The point is, bird mothers have been caring for their babies for millions of years. They're smart, compassionate, and loving. Your child can help best by getting out of the way and giving Mother Bird room to get the job done. Always respect a mother's wisdom.

75. How to Skip a Rock

A positive, happy attitude is like a skipping stone; it will carry you lightly over deep water.

—A Good Dad Saying

An ordinary kid beside a pond or lake will throw a rock in the water and enjoy the *ker-PLUNK!* But if that kid has an adventurous spirit, those *ker-PLUNKS* will soon change to *chit! chit! chit!* as he skips one rock after another across the wide, sylvan pool. If a kindred soul appears, they'll soon be competing to see who can make the most skips with one rock.

And if one of these free spirits happens to be your kid, he'll garner the championship hands down. Why? Because you've taught your protégé the three secrets of rock skipping: get a flat rock, put a spin on it, and throw it at a low angle. With these three bits of dad knowledge, your kid can get one-two-three-four-five-six-seven-eight or more skips out of one rock.

To get the right spin, have him hold the rock in the crotch of his thumb and forefinger, with his forefinger curved around the edge of the rock (see figure.) Then have him face the pool, bend sideways, and throw side-armed. As he releases the stone, it should be spinning and on a low-angle trajectory to the water's surface. Spinning causes more of the rock to hit the water, so it acts flatter than it really is. And hitting the water at a low angle conserves energy, so the rock will have more for the next skip. By throwing this way, he'll get nice, long skips, like those of a gazelle bounding in the sunshine.

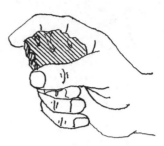

Skipping rocks is more fun than watching Saturday morning cartoons, and your child can learn a lot about the dynamics of nature from those little rock leaps. When NASA scientists first designed the Space Shuttle, they considered slowing down the craft as it returned from space by skipping it across the Earth's atmosphere *much as a rock is skipped across a pond.* There's more meaning in nature than we comprehend. And the more time a child spends in nature, even playfully skipping rocks, the more likely he is to understand.

76. How to Identify a Bird

Birds are easy to identify. Common egrets look dumb enough not to know who they are, and American coots act mean enough not to give their real names. But we know them all.

—A Good Dad Reflection

Children uneducated in bird lore are at a loss when they see birds in the wild. On a walk through the woods, an American pipit is "just a sparrow," a common house finch with its cranberry-red breast is a "redbird," and a white crowned sparrow is "maybe some new kind of bird."

But you can clear up your kid's confusion, because you know birds are identified by certain categories. Once your child knows where a bird fits into these five categories, he's well on his way to naming it:

Habitat: Is the bird a swimmer or a wader? Is he seen only in the mountains or mostly in the desert?

Size. Is he large or small? Estimate his size in inches.

Coloration: This is an easy one, and knowing these first three factors may be enough to identify the bird. A very large bird with an all-white neck and head, seen in the mountains, would be a bald eagle. There's no other bird like that in the mountains. On the prairie, a medium-size bird, all yellow with a solid black V-shaped breast band, would have to be a meadowlark.

Bill shape: Look to see if it's the large, seed-cracking bill of a finch; the long, needle-like beak of a warbler; or the hooked beak of a small hawk.

Field marks: Does the bird have wing bars? Is his breast striped, speckled, or plain? How about his tail and rump? Does he have eye lines?

There are many subtleties to identifying birds. Ornithologists devote their lives to this pursuit. But these five categories along with a good field guide will get your kid started. They'll also keep him from being one of those people who, at the end of their lives, realize they walked by the little, beautiful things and never saw them.

77. How to Pass a Soccer Ball

Learning to play soccer is a lot like learning gymnastics with the gym secured to the open bed of an eighteen-wheeler doing seventy miles per hour down the interstate.

—A Good Dad Observation

Soccer players do everything on the move. Unable to stop and think, a kid has to pass on the run, with two defensemen at his elbows and another trying to kick the ball. No wonder most beginners' passes spray like buckshot all over the field.

Fortunately, you know the way your kid can keep moving and still control his passes. He should use the inside of his foot and think of it as a golf club. If he wants to pass to his right, he should kick with the inside of his left foot. To pass to a player on his left, he should kick with his right foot.

To teach him how to make this pass, have him place his nonkicking foot about four inches from the ball, with his toes pointed in the direction he wants to pass and his knee slightly bent. Then have him strike the ball with the flat inside part of his kicking foot. If you play golf, you know that to make the ball travel far, you have to hit it slightly below center. The same holds true in soccer. If your kid wants distance, he should strike the ball slightly below center. For short-range passes that stay low, he should swing his foot just slightly off the ground so it strikes the center of the ball. To make his passes smooth, encourage him to make sure he "follows through" with his foot even after the ball is in the air.

To practice, have your kid mount a target on a wall or garage door. Then have him aim for this target until he can hit it accurately from five, ten, or even fifteen feet away.

As your child learns to stand calmly in the heat of battle and pass a soccer ball smoothly, he'll also learn the value of keeping his balance in a hectic, stressful moment. And that's not a bad lesson for life.

DAD TIP

Balance: The Key to Good Soccer Play

When your kid watches pro soccer players, he'll notice they always run with their arms outstretched like they're trying to fly. Why? To keep their balance. Even when struggling for the ball, good players keep their hands up. Teach your child this trick, and he'll become a better, safer player.

---

78. How to Read a Compass

A compass, like a strong guiding principle, will see you through lots of troubles.

—Good Dad Wisdom

High country or desert outings are lots of fun. But what if a kid wanders away from camp? Even if she has a global positioning system (GPS) receiver, that only tells her *where* she is. How can she tell which direction to walk?

Well, of course, you know the device that will always keep her from getting lost: the compass. And the secret to helping her understand this device is that bobbing red needle inside. The earth is a giant magnet, and this needle is magnetized. So no matter where your child is—on the whole earth—this needle always points north. It's her rock of stability in a confusing, uncertain world.

To introduce your child to an orienteering compass:

1. Show her that all-important red needle, which always points north (see figure).

2. Call her attention to the dial of numbers around the outside edge of the compass. Called the "azimuth ring," this dial is marked off in directions (north, east, south, west) and broken into degrees (360 of them). In fact, azimuth literally means "direction" or "bearing."

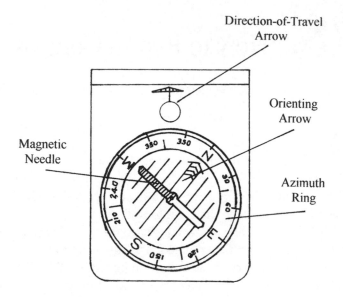

Direction-of-Travel Arrow

Orienting Arrow

Magnetic Needle

Azimuth Ring

3. Now have her notice the orienting arrow on the inside floor of the compass. When she rotates this arrow until it's under the red needle, both point north. Then all the other directions on the azimuth ring also point accurately to east, south, and west.

4. Finally, have her observe the direction-of-travel arrow. She should always point this arrow the direction she's walking. Then she'll always stay on the same course. She can also point this arrow at some landmark (like a tower or mountain) to determine which direction she needs to walk to get there.

As your child journeys through life, she'll confront many choices. And when she does, she may remember the lesson of the compass: in an uncertain world, she can always rely on true principles to guide her down the right path.

DAD FACT

Magnetic versus True North

Magnetic north is not true north. That's because the magnetic north pole is in Canada, 1,200 miles away from the true North Pole. The difference between the two norths is called "declination." Because of this declination, the magnetic needle on your child's compass may point as much as twenty degrees westerly in Maine or thirty degrees easterly in Alaska. On a line running through Wisconsin and the western panhandle of Florida, magnetic north and true north are the same.

---

79. How to Find Your Way with a Compass

We should always know the direction our moral compass points and make sure we've set the right course.

—A Good Dad Maxim

Your child already knows how to read a compass (see chapter 78). He's got all those numbers, dials, and arrows down pat. But a compass without a destination is like a basketball without a hoop. With no goal to aim for, there's no challenge. To let your child test his compass-reading skills, you've decided to take him on a day hike and let him find his way cross country to some destination—like a small lake over the hills and through the woods.

To keep it simple, let's assume you've already figured out the lake is due west from your position on the trail. Now have your kid adjust the compass, lining up the orienting arrow and the needle so the directions on the dial match those in the real world. Next, have your child hold the compass against his chest and point the direction-of-travel arrow due west. That's the direction you're going to walk.

Let's suppose you see that the direction-of-travel arrow is pointing directly at a large rock on a hilltop. Walk to that rock. From the hilltop, you see a woods spread across a valley below.

Keeping his same compass settings, have your child gaze across the valley to the next hill and pick out some landmark—perhaps a distinctive tree—at which the direction-of-travel arrow is pointing. This landmark should be highly visible, so he can still see it while you're in the woods. Walk toward that object. When you reach the tree, you both look down in the second valley, and there's your lake. Your kid has found his way cross-country to a lake he couldn't even see.

To retrace your steps, simply have your child rotate the compass dial 180 degrees. To do this, he should hold the direction-of-travel arrow steady on the bearing you've been walking. Then have him rotate the dial so the orienting arrow aligns with the south end of the magnetic needle. Now he should turn the whole compass so the orienting arrow is aligned with the north end of the magnetic needle. The direction-of-travel arrow now points the way back to your car.

DAD TIP

Orienting a Map to the Real World

In the bottom margin of most topographical maps, your kid will find an angle with one leg marked true north and the other marked magnetic north. To orient the map—so that north on the map points to north in the real world—have your child lay the compass on this angle, so that the magnetic needle on the compass lines up with magnetic north on the map. All directions on the map now correspond to the directions in the real world.

As you head back toward civilization, you might observe that life sometimes mimics this rugged country he's just crossed. It's often hard to see where one's going. But with trustworthy principles to guide him, he'll never get lost.

80. How to Get a Close-up Look at a Snowflake

Forget what "everybody else" is doing. God made you to be an original.
—Good Dad Wisdom

Snowflakes are fleeting bits of reality. Most kids have heard no two snowflakes are alike. But let a child try to capture a snowflake, and it melts away before she can see it. So during the next snowfall, treat your child to a good close-up look at a snowflake.

The secret: use chilled black velvet. When a snowflake lands on anything hard (even black paper), it tends to flatten out. Ice-cold velvet catches snow so softly the flake retains its perfect six-sided, three-dimensional shape.

Here's how your child can make the perfect snowflake catcher. First have her take an eight-by-one-inch board and saw eight inches off of one end (see chapter 4, "How to Saw a Board"). When she finishes, she'll have a piece of wood eight inches square. Then with carpet tacks, have her tack black velvet onto the board (see chapter 64, "How to Use a Hammer"). Now have her chill the velvet, either by setting it outside in a sheltered spot where it can't get covered with snow, or putting it in the freezer of your refrigerator.

During a snowstorm, have her stand outside and catch several falling flakes on the velvet. With a magnifying glass, she can then study each flake separately. So long as the flakes don't pile on top of each other, she'll be able to note the infinite variety. She can also shine a bright flashlight on the crystals, then observe the fascinating ways the light reflects off different shapes. She'll soon see for herself that each flake in its lacy beauty is, indeed, one of a kind.

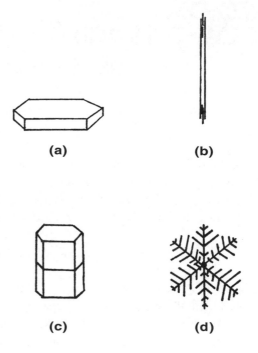

(a) **(b)** **(c)** **(d)**

As she marvels at the complexity of snow, you can point out that God made people a lot like He made snowflakes; we're all alike in some ways. But a closer look reveals that each one of us is an original.

How Cold Are the Clouds?

Though each snowflake is unique, the crystals from which they're formed come in only four basic shapes: the six-sided plate, the six-pointed star, the six-sided column, and the needle. The temperature in the cloud where it forms determines the shape a crystal will take. So by examining the crystals in a snowflake, your child can literally tell how cold the clouds are overhead.

Temperatures from 32° to 27° Fahrenheit form plates (figure a), 27° to 23° form needles (figure b), 23° to 18° form columns (figure c), 18° to −13° form plates again, −13° to −58° form columns. Dendrites (which resemble stars, figure d) are formed between 10° and 3°, but usually only if there's lots of wind. A snowflake, being a puffball collection of crystals, may contain several of these shapes.

81. How to Win a Chess Game in Two Moves

In chess, as in life, close the deal as fast as you can.

—A Good Dad Motto

Once they grasp the rules, kids find chess fascinating. Viewing chess as a type of IQ test, they love to "out-think" their opponent. But chess is so complicated that most kids soon get distracted. They shilly-shally around the board, trying to think fifteen or twenty moves ahead, letting the game drag on for hours. They entirely lose sight of their goal: to checkmate the king.

Fortunately, there's a fast way to help your child become a better chess player. How? Show him how to win a game in only two moves.

This sequence is called "fool's mate" because it requires two foolish moves by his opponent. Here's how it works:

Move #1: Your kid's opponent (playing white—white always moves first) opens by moving a bishop's pawn one space. Your kid (playing black) responds by moving his king pawn two spaces (figure a).

Move #2: The other kid, thinking the game has "just begun," fails to see the obvious right in front of his eyes. He moves his knight's pawn two spaces (figure b).

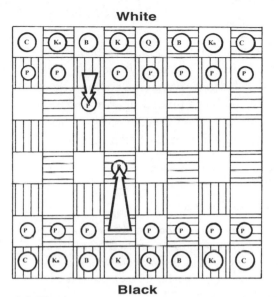

White

Black

(a) First move

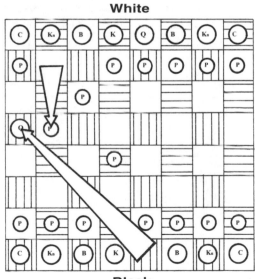

White

**(b) Second
move—
black check-
mates white**

Black

Seizing the initiative, your kid doesn't hesitate; he moves his queen to the square shown (figure b), and "Checkmate!" He wins. He'll have learned to keep his eye on the goal and checkmate as soon as he can. At the same time, he'll learn that thinking too far ahead can be a waste of his time. Success in chess, as in life, means thinking clearly about the situation right now.

DAD TIP

Getting Serious about Chess

Fool's mate is a fun way for a kid to show off. But, of course, anyone who wants to learn the intricacies of chess and play in tournaments needs to work hard. In chess, there should be a purpose behind every move a kid makes. One of the best books for beginners is *Logical Chess: Move by Move* by Irving Chernev (Dulles, Va.: Brassey's Inc., 1999). You can also find out lots about chess clubs and tournaments on the Internet.

---

82. How to Change the Oil in a Car

E. B. White had it right: "Everything in life is somewhere else, and you get there in a car." So you'd better know how to change the oil.
—Good Dad Wisdom

Your child has no interest in the car. When you go out to check the coolant or the spark plugs, she suddenly becomes busy with a phone call to a friend. Yet you know she'll be driving this car one day, and she should take some interest in it. Changing the oil together is one good way to make her think about the effort it takes to keep a car in good working order.

Tell her there's a secret to changing the oil: the front end of the car should be raised. To do this, she'll need to use those heavy steel ramps sold in any auto parts store. (She should never jack up the car to change the oil because if the jack slips, the falling car could seriously hurt her if she's under it.)

Supporting the front wheels with the ramps, she should then set the emergency brake and chock the back wheels. Oil runs better when it's warm, so warm up the motor by letting it run a couple of minutes. Now remove the oil-filter cap, and slide under the car. If you don't want to get your hands dirty, wear neoprene gloves.

The oil pan is the metal cover on the bottom of the engine. At the back of the oil pan is a large plug that looks like a bolt. Remove this plug with a socket wrench. If you want your kid to do this part, give her a breaker bar (a long handle for the wrench), so she'll have enough leverage to do it. She should pull the plug away quickly, so oil won't run over her hand. Let the oil drain into a wide, shallow pan you've placed under the drain. Once the oil has drained, replace the plug and tighten it down with the wrench. Shift the pan so it's under the oil filter.

Now scoot out from under the car. Using a filter wrench, loosen the oil filter on the side of the engine, and unscrew the filter the rest of the way by hand. But be careful; you ran the engine for a while, so the manifold may be hot. Also, the filter's full of old, dirty oil. So once it's removed, tilt it up immediately so oil won't spill all over everything.

Check your owner's manual to make sure you have the right filter. Rub a coating of the oil you're going to use onto the rubber gasket of the new filter. Screw the filter on by hand about three-fourths of a turn until it's firmly tightened. Don't use a filer wrench because overtightening the filter will damage the gasket.

Refill the engine with the correct oil as specified in your owner's manual. Dispose of the old oil by pouring it in a container, which you'll take to a recycling center that accepts used oil.

Changing the oil in a car can be a messy business. But as you wipe that smudge off your kid's nose and order out for pizza, you'll know you've taught her a lot about the way a car works. Since we depend so much on cars, there's no telling when that might come in handy.

83. How to Signal SOS

Independence is a good thing, but never be afraid to ask for help when you need it.

—A Good Dad Adage

With all the satellite guidance systems now in place, knowing how to signal SOS could be a dad skill on the verge of extinction. The equivalent of SOS today is 911. Yet anytime a kid's in danger and without a phone—let's say she's lost in the woods or the desert—she needs to know this basic skill. It could save her life.

As a good dad knows, SOS comes from the old International Code used by telegraph operators. This universal cry for help is simply three dots (...), followed by three dashes (- - -), followed by three dots (...). Tell your child she can use this "code" anytime she's desperate for help and in any number of ways. Examples:

Three short, loud tweets on a whistle, followed by three long tweets, followed by three short tweets.

Three short, rapid flashes from a flashlight, followed by three long, slow flashes, followed by three short, rapid flashes.

Three short honks of a car horn, followed by three long honks, followed by three short honks.

Three short, rapid knocks on a wall, followed by three, slow, hard, deliberate pounds, followed by three short, rapid knocks.

Teach her the variations are endless and limited only by her imagination. You'll feel safer knowing she has this versatile skill. And she'll feel more protected, knowing that in an emergency, she's prepared.

84. How to Tie a Necktie

There's no sense putting on a tie to look good if you're going to tie it sloppy.

— A Good Dad Saying

For most boys, learning how to tie a necktie is a kind of initiation into manhood. Girls today also often need to know this skill. Yet when kids attempt tying a tie on their own, they often get it so wadded up and askance, they wind up looking worse than when they started.

As a good dad knows, there are several correct ways to knot a necktie. But this method produces an especially smooth, tidy knot called the Windsor knot. The secret in any case is to start with the fat side at least twice as long as the skinny side.

1. Have your child start with the tie looped around his neck, *inside out*, the long, fat side on his right and the short, skinny side on his left.

2. Cross the skinny side of the tie across the fat side (figure a).

3. Now cross the fat side across the skinny side (figure b).

4. Then bring the thick part of the tie up through the hole between the tie and the neck (figure c).

5. Now put the tie down through the small loop as shown (figure d).

6. Tighten the tie by pulling down on the skinny end in the back, and adjust the knot until it looks great.

This skill is so simple it may seem hardly worth teaching. But it's a dad's job. And if you don't do it, who will? In this age of informality, we've heard of grown men who can't tie a tie. Mark Twain was right when he said, "Be careless in your dress if you must, but keep a tidy soul." Yet it's also as true today as it was in the seventeenth century when cleric Thomas Fuller first said it, "Good clothes open all doors."

(a)

(b)

(c)

(d)

85. How to Make Kindling

When you think you've exhausted all possibilities, remember this: you haven't.

—A Good Dad Saying

Most kids go camping just for the campfire. They love the open, crackling flame, the flickering, dancing light. It's a sterile, cheerless camp when the wood's wet and a fire won't start, like no popcorn at the movies. As kids futilely search the forest floor for dry sticks to start a fire, they may dismally conclude the situation's hopeless.

But you know the fun's not done. That's because you know where there's always plenty of dry kindling to start a big, roaring fire. Wood, you tell your child, is waterproof. Unless it's green or rotten, it's only wet on the outside. Inside the large chunks, it's always dry.

To get to this dry kindling, have your child select one or two straight, knotless logs from your supply of campfire wood. If he can't find knotless sticks, he should choose those with as few small knots as possible. Now here's how to split the wood almost into splinters:

1. Hold a log on the ground upright, and position the cutting edge of the hatchet on the top of the stick, exactly where you want the wood to split.

2. Holding the hatchet and the end of the stick of wood together, lift both, then swing them down against the ground with a gentle, tapping motion. Don't strike hard enough to split the wood. Just tap gently enough to set the hatchet blade in the log.

3. With the hatchet imbedded in the wood, grasp the handle with both hands and strike the end of the log hard against the ground. The hatchet will drive like a wedge into the log, splitting it in two.

4. Repeat steps 1–3, creating several thin slabs of wood. Then position the hatchet crosswise each slab and make as much fine kindling as you want.

In a few minutes, the two of you will have a cozy fire blazing. And from now on, each time your kid chops kindling, he'll be reminded it's not enough to skim over the surface of things. To get to the good stuff—whether in wood or in people—you often have to look deeper.

DAD SAFETY TIP

Never sharpen an ax or a hatchet to a fine cutting edge. Both are designed as wedges to force wood apart, not as cutting tools in place of a saw or a knife.

86. How to Build a Campfire

Building a campfire is a bit like starting civilization from scratch.
—A Good Dad Saying

It's the end of a long day in the car. For the last two hours, your child has been looking forward to this evening's campfire. But when you arrive at your campground, the only other campers are disconsolately cooking over a camp stove. "We couldn't get a fire started," one camper complains. As you head off to set up your own camp, your concerned child asks, "Can *we* start a fire?"

"Sure," you reply, without hesitation. "We have a butane lighter to provide an open flame, the woods to supply us with fuel, and the air to provide oxygen. With those three elements, a fire has to burn."

As you collect firewood, you explain the secret to building a campfire: always leave plenty of cracks between the wood for the oxygen to pass through. Fires fail to start usually because the wood is blocking the flow of oxygen. If oxygen can't get to the flame, the fire goes out. It's snuffed out as surely as if she'd thrown a shovel of dirt on it. So tell your child she always needs to leave a clear path for air flow.

To illustrate this, show her how to construct a campfire like a log cabin with cracks between the logs (see figure). Tiny splinters and other tinder go inside the cabin. Once the cabin's complete, ignite the tinder with your butane lighter. Then add a "roof" with two layers of sticks, leaving cracks for the air to pass through.

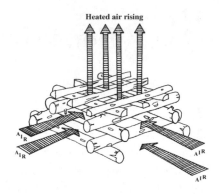

As the flame heats the air inside the log cabin, the air rises, creating a vacuum. Fresh air is then drawn into the cabin's central room through the cracks in the walls. As the air flows into the cabin, the wood burns brighter and hotter.

As the fire builds, you and your child can add bigger and bigger sticks until you have a large, hearty flame. Then while you sit toasting hot dogs, you can remind your kid that civilization, like this fire you just started, is the end result of acquired skills.

DAD TIP

You wouldn't try today to catch all your food in the wild, use a flat rock to make pancakes, or drink lake water as is. So why scrounge for dry tinder? Next time you go camping, try fire starter. A clear paste that comes in a toothpaste-like tube, fire starter comes in several brands and is sold in most sporting-goods stores. Your kid just squeezes some into the bottom of the campfire structure where she'd put regular tinder, ignites it with a butane lighter, and instantly has a fire.

87. How to Slide into Second

Perseverance is the hard work you do after you've given one hundred percent.

—A Good Dad Saying

When kids watch ballplayers sliding into bases on TV, they think it looks easy. No problem. You just fall down and slide. But you know if a kid slides wrong into a base, she could twist an ankle or get a baseman's knee in her face.

So teach your kid the safest way to slide into a base. The secret is to start with the figure-four slide. There are many different slides, from the head-first to the hook. But the figure four is a good beginner slide. It's safe. It will enable her to avoid the tag. And it will immediately bring her back to her feet, ready to run on to the next base.

First, make sure she has the right footwear: running shoes or sneakers, never cleats. Catching a cleat in the grass or ground could seriously twist her ankle. Stress that once she starts into a slide, she needs to go through with it smoothly. Changing her mind in the middle of a slide results in a jerky motion that could get her hurt.

As she starts into her slide, she'll literally sit down with her right leg extended toward the base. Her left leg will be tucked under the right one, giving her body the look of a figure four (which is, of course, where this slide got its name). She slides to the base on her tucked-in leg and hip pockets.

As she slides, make sure she keeps her right leg slightly flexed. Like a shock absorber, the slightly flexed leg absorbs the impact of ramming into the base, and thereby prevents injuries. She should hold both hands above her shoulders as she slides so she won't scrape her knuckles or jam a finger.

At the end of the slide, have her stand quickly by lifting herself with her tucked-under leg. As she rises to her feet, she'll immediately be facing home plate. That's why you had her tuck under her left leg. (If she'd tucked under her right leg, she'd now be facing center or left field.)

Encourage your child to practice this slide so often that by the time she gets to a game, it's just second nature. Then, in the heat of the moment, she can trust her instincts. By not having to hesitate as she gets up, she'll gain an advantage. And in a competitive sport like baseball, every honest advantage used puts her that much closer to winning.

88. How to Identify Six Animal Tracks

You can learn a lot from wild animal tracks. They never go to the mall.
— A Good Dad Observation

Since most children on a hike never see a deer or mountain lion, they think there are no animals in the woods. They fail to realize how crafty wild beasts are at remaining unseen. So teach your child to read wild animal signs.

If you find bear tracks, the bear was there. Once you know what to look for, you can show your child where the bear stopped for water, prowled around an old log, or even stood on his hind legs to look curiously around. And not only big animals delight kids. You could also track a raccoon to its den.

When looking for tracks, you might first search the mud around a stream or lake. With luck, you'll spot a few of these:

Domestic dog (figure a): Very commonly seen on hiking trails and easy to confuse with the coyote, the dog has an almost circular track. You can see the claws on all four toes. This track is usually accompanied by human footprints.

Bobcat (figure b): The more rounded cat print also has four toes, but the claws *don't* show. The tracks of a bobcat, lynx, and mountain lion are a lot alike, except for the size. The bobcat's track is about 2 to 2½ inches across, the lynx's about 3 to

(a) Domestic dog

(b) Bobcat

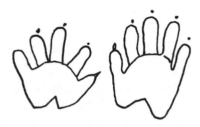

(c) Raccoon

(d) Opossum

(e) Bear

(f) Coyote

$3\frac{1}{2}$ inches, and the lion's about $3\frac{1}{4}$ to $4\frac{1}{4}$ inches wide. A pet cat, in contrast, has a track only 1 to $1\frac{3}{4}$ inches across.

Raccoon (figure c): The raccoon's print, often found near water and about 2 to 3 inches long, looks like a baby walked by on his hands. It has five long, finger-like toes—all pointing straight ahead—with claws at the tips.

Opossum (figure d): This track looks similar to a raccoon's, except it has an *opposable* thumb. The "thumb" on the hind foot has no claw. Opossum tracks are 7 to 14 inches apart, with the hind track overlapping the front.

Bear (figure e): Bears have five toes on their front and back feet, with long nails on their front paws that leave imprints in the ground. If it's a black bear, its nails are shorter than its toes. If it's a grizzly, they're longer.

Coyote (figure f): The coyote's print looks much like a domestic dog's, with two important differences. The coyote track tends to be more oval-shaped, with only two claws on the front toes, pointed inward. The two claws on the back toes usually don't show.

Children so seldom see animals in the wild that the woods must seem inhabited by rumors. But once your child learns to read their signs, he'll suddenly find the woods full of animals and their activities. Understanding a wild animal's signs is like reading its diary for the day.

89. How–and Where– to Dig for Clams

The best vision is insight.
    —Malcolm S. Forbes, the Good Dad of *Forbes* Magazine

You're vacationing near an ocean bay, where you've heard the clamming is great. One day your kid shouts with delight, "Hey! Let's have a clambake." At this point, most parents would pile their eager offspring in the car, drive to a fish market, and buy clams—or even just go to a restaurant. But, as a good dad, you know how proud and self-sufficient a kid feels when he can catch his own food.

Besides, you know a secret about clamming most people don't. You know how to look in the sand near the high-water mark for a bunch of small holes, like someone's been poking nails in the shore.

Clams, at least the soft-shelled kind, have a strange habit: they squirt saltwater to create air holes in the sand, so they can breathe. Under each of these telltale holes, your kid should find a clam. Tell him to watch closely, and he may even see a small geyser of water shoot out of a hole. Then he'll be sure there's a clam hiding below.

Once your kid has found clams, the rest is simple. Just have him dig them up with a pitch fork. But he might want to steer clear, or he could get saltwater sprayed in his face! Then have him carefully wash the sand off the clams, plop them in a bucket, and take them back to the cabin for dinner.

Your kid can find a different kind of clam—the hard-shelled quahog (great for chowder)—by rolling up his pant legs, wading into the shallow water barefoot, and feeling around in the bottom of the bay with his toes. When his foot touches something that feels like a small rock, have him reach down in the mud with his hand. If he's lucky, he'll pull up a quahog. If he pulls up a rock, have him hurl it far out in the water so he won't get fooled by that same rock twice.

Catching clams can be great sport, and it teaches your kid some of the best things in life are free. Many rewards—even a delicacy like a delicious clam dinner—can be his for the taking, if he'll just keep his eyes open.

DAD FACT

When to Go Clamming

The very best time for clamming is a day or two before a full moon. That's when the tides are at their lowest, exposing more of the bay bottom, where the juicy little morsels hide.

90. How to Hold a Puppy

The dog was created specially for children. He is the god of frolic.
—Henry Ward Beecher,
Minister and a Good Dad of Abolitionism

With his big, wet, soulful eyes and naturally curious nature, a puppy simply begs, "Pick me up." Every kid wants to cuddle that cute bundle of fur with the wet, slurpy tongue. But a puppy handled wrong can become frightened or get his feelings hurt. When a mother dog chastises her puppy, for instance, she lifts him by the scruff of the neck and shakes it. So a puppy picked up this way feels humiliated.

Fortunately, you can easily teach your child how to pick up a puppy so he'll feel happy and safe.

First, she should ask the owner if it's okay to handle the dog. But once the owner says yes, she should ask the puppy. How? Have her offer the puppy the back of her hand to sniff. If he wags his tail and wiggles or otherwise invites her to play, then she's welcome to pick him up.

To make the puppy feel secure, show your child how to slide one hand in under his tummy, then forward between his front legs. Her fingertips should rest under the puppy's chest, with her palm under his rib cage. Then have her cup the dog's bottom with her other hand and lift. The puppy will soon forget all fears of being hurt or humiliated and start to enjoy being held.

As you watch your child laugh and get a good face washing from that ever-present tongue, you'll know she's also learning that love and gentleness always go hand in hand.

DAD FACT

When Shyness Is a Warning Sign

Be wary of any puppy who's unduly shy. If he slinks away or tries to crawl under a chair to avoid being held, tell your child to leave him alone. He might fear-bite. Although it rarely happens, a few dogs develop neurotic fears of strangers. The owner, who's no stranger to the dog, may be unaware of the problem. But these overly timid dogs do bite, even if their owners insist that they don't.

91.

How to Get a Close Look at a Bird While It's Nesting

To learn facts about birds nobody else knows, look at them in ways nobody else does.

—A Good Dad Maxim

Most kids who love birds are happy with an ordinary backyard bird feeder or birdhouse. But to encourage your child's enthusiasm for the little winged creatures, you want to go the extra mile. With a unique birdhouse like the one you're about to build, it's as good as having the bird's nest in your child's room.

Use a two-way mirror for one wall of the house, and then mount the house on your kid's bedroom window. She can watch the birds for hours, and they won't even know she's there.

Buy a two-way mirror that measures 6 × 8¾ inches. Then to build the house, look at the blueprint (see figure) and follow these steps:

1. Cut out the pieces of the birdhouse. You'll need one 9 × 9-inch piece cut from ¼-inch all-weather plywood (the roof); two 1 × 6 × 10-inch pieces (the side walls); one 1 × 6 × 7-inch piece (the bottom of the birdhouse); and one 1 × 4 × 7-inch piece (the front wall).

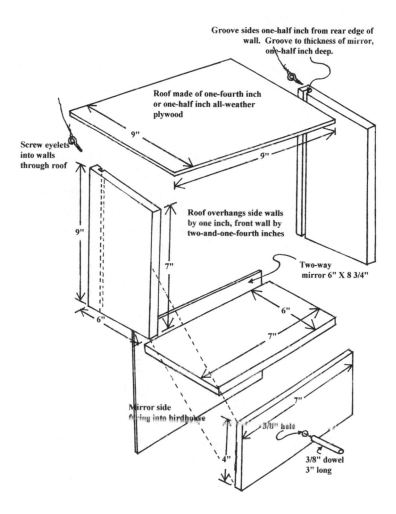

Groove sides one-half inch from rear edge of wall. Groove to thickness of mirror, one-half inch deep.

Roof made of one-fourth inch or one-half inch all-weather plywood

9"

9"

Screw eyelets into walls through roof

Roof overhangs side walls by one inch, front wall by two-and-one-fourth inches

9"

7"

Two-way mirror 6" X 8 3/4"

6"

6"

7"

Mirror side fitting into birdhouse

7"

3/8" hole

4"

3/8" dowel 3" long

217

2. Take the two side walls. Cut a slant across each wall so the wall will be 9 inches deep at the top and 7 inches deep at the bottom (see figure).

3. Now groove the side walls, as shown, so you can slip the mirror between them. Cut each groove the thickness of the mirror, or just about the thickness of a saw blade. Make sure the two grooves will be facing each other when the walls are in place in the birdhouse.

4. Drill a ⅜-inch hole in the front wall, as shown, and drive a ⅜-inch dowel, 3 inches long, into this hole.

5. Now you're ready to assemble the house. Assemble the pieces in this order: nail roof to side walls; nail front wall to side walls; slide mirror in place (make sure the mirror side is facing into the birdhouse); and nail bottom in place.

6. Finally screw two eyelets into the side walls through the roof as shown and hang the birdhouse by wires in front of your child's bedroom window.

With a two-way mirror, just one reminder; if it's dark in front of the mirror (as it will be on a dark night) and light behind (as it will be if your kid has the lights on in her room), the bird can see your child, get frightened, and abandon the nest. So when your child's in her room, have her keep a piece of paper taped across the mirror, and tell her not to lift it until it's daylight outside. Even then, she should make sure her room lights are off.

With an original birdhouse like this, your kid will get to watch birds up close in their natural habitat. She'll also learn that we make our own opportunities. Sometimes we just have to build our own windows to see them.

92. How to Find a Fossil

The guy who finds a fossil is the one who keeps hunting after everybody else has gone home.

—A Good Dad Observation

Once they hear about dinosaurs, kids often develop a passion for fossils. Imagine finding a stegosaurus tooth or the remains of a plant that was green when tyrannosaurus rex stomped the earth. Told fossils can be "anywhere" (they could be, but so could gold), kids begin eagerly examining every rock they see, only to be disappointed.

But you know how your kid can find a fossil and retain his enthusiasm for prehistory. Look in limestone. That's where nearly all fossils are found. Forget all those other rocks.

You can explain that there are three kinds of rocks on Earth: igneous, metamorphic, and sedimentary. Igneous and metamorphic are formed under intense heat or pressure and yield very few fossils. Sedimentary rocks, primarily limestone, sandstone, and shale, are made from the remains of plants, algae, shells, and other organisms. To find these fossil-rich sedimentary rocks, tell your kid to focus on streambeds, cliffs, rocky outcroppings, caves, quarries, tunnels, canals, railway or road cuts—anyplace the earth has been cut away by man or the winds.

Choose a sunny day and wear old clothes. Take along a hammer, one or two cold chisels, a magnifying glass, an old pocketknife, newspaper, soft tissues, labels, pens, a notebook, and various jars, cans, and small boxes. Goggles (important) will protect your kid's eyes from flying rock chips as he whacks the rocks. If you can find a trustworthy "where-to-hunt fossils" pamphlet put out by your local geology society, so much the better.

Once you have a good fossil location, work the area carefully. Mentally divide the ground into grids, and go over every square foot. Your kid will need to crawl on his hands and knees and put his nose almost up to the rocks. Direct "front" light can make a fossil hard to see, so have your child study rocks with light coming from the side or even in from behind the rock. Also, have him look for an ant mound. Since ants gather rocks and other small-fossil-containing particles, they may have done his work for him.

While fossil hunting can be a great adventure, it also helps develop strong character habits. In the end your kid will succeed by observing three rules: (1) don't give up, (2) keep trying, and (3) try again.

DAD TIP

The Fizz Test

To tell whether a rock is limestone, your kid can simply drop some vinegar or soda water on it. If it's limestone, it will fizz. Why? The vinegar or soda reacts with a material in limestone called carbonate to produce tiny bubbles of carbon dioxide gas. The fizzing is the sound of these little bubbles popping. He can also give his rock the "scratch test." Limestone will scratch with a knife, but not with a fingernail or a penny.

93. How to Straighten a Nail

A mistake corrected is a mistake not made.

—A Good Dad Saying

There's something about starting a project that makes a kid want to finish it. It's frustrating to start over again, even if he's just bent a nail. But what can he do? If he tries to straighten the nail by tapping it with a hammer, he'll only bend it anew where it enters the board.

Well, of course, you know the solution is in the claws of the hammer. A hammer is a great deal like a pencil. There's the part you do business with on one end and the part for correcting mistakes—the claws—on the other. Usually, claws only pull out nails. But they can also straighten a bent one. You might want to teach your child this skill when he's learning to hammer. That's when he'll bend lots of nails.

1. Have him put the claws around the nail—where it's bent—and jam the nail deep into the V.

2. He should twist the hammer sideways. If the nail's bent to the right, he should twist to the left. If it's bent to the left, he should twist to the right. He may not get the nail perfectly straight, but he can probably get it straight enough to continue driving. And once the nail goes into the wood past the bend, it won't bend again.

3. Your child can also straighten a crooked nail by laying it—hump up—on any flat, metal surface (like an anvil). Have him lay the nail head over the edge of the metal. Then as he holds the nail with a pair of pliers in one hand, he can hammer it flat with the other hand.

Once the nail is straight again, your kid should still hammer it carefully. Why? Because once bent, a nail will bend at the same place again with the slightest bad blow. There's a lesson here, of course, for all of life. With a little effort, we can usually straighten out our mistakes. But our characters are all too frequently like that nail: the slightest bad blow life delivers makes us bend in the same place again.

94. How to Whistle with a Blade of Grass

There's more music in nature than the wind whistling through the willows.

—A Good Dad Maxim

As children increasingly grow up in cities, far from pastures and meadows, the ability to make a blade of grass sing is slowly but surely being lost. Yet a child taught this classic dad skill learns the joy of relying on his own resources for entertainment. She can also show off to her friends.

The trick is to start with the right blade of grass. Forget all those soft, velvety blades that carpet well-manicured lawns. Your kid wants a nice weedy piece of grass, a rather wide strand that will stand firm and vibrate musically when she blows on it.

Have your child start by holding the blade between her thumbs, where the thumbs meet the heels of her hand. Then have her catch the blade again higher up, right above the first joint (see figure). Some whistlers like to scooch the blade into this position. However she does it, she needs to stretch the blade tautly across that little long, thin opening between the base of her thumbs. Note that the opening looks a bit like the mouthpiece of a flute. And the grass blade resembles a musical reed. This is her instrument.

Now have her blow gently on the grass to make it vibrate. It can be tough at first to get a sound, but encourage her to persist. Eventually, the blade will start buzzing as merrily as a cricket on a warm summer night. Learning to whistle through a blade of grass teaches dexterity and the rewards of diligent effort. It also teaches a child that many opportunities we overlook in life secretly contain hidden music. We often just need to know how to bring it out.

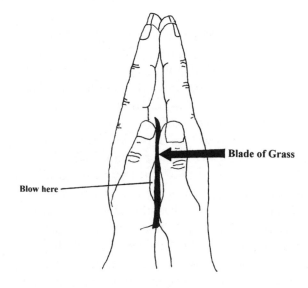

Blade of Grass

Blow here

95. How to Perform in a Clutch

Some men break under pressure, others break records.
            —A Good Dad Aphorism

It's the bottom of the ninth. Your kid is pitching with two on and two out. His team is up by only one run. *Or . . .* your kid's basketball team is down by one point. There's just one second left on the clock, and your kid is at the free throw line. In either case, everybody on the opposing team is screaming, "You're going to blow it, turkey! You're going to looosssssseeee!!!" They're wildly waving their arms, throwing towels, anything to shake your kid up.

Most kids in this situation would have "rabbit ears." They'd hear all the criticism, get rattled, and blow the game. But your kid wings his fast ball past the batter for "Strike three!" or hits the hoop with a swisher.

What does he know about performing in a clutch that most kids don't? He knows how to avoid rabbit ears. The secret: no one can think about two things at the same time. If your kid concentrates hard enough on making that pitch or shooting that basket, he can't even hear his opponents' razzing. It just becomes meaningless background noise.

Teaching your kid to avoid rabbit ears requires preparing him for this situation early. Tell him to expect criticism and not take it personally. It's just part of the other team's defense, as normal as an opposing player trying to catch a pop fly or block a shot.

Tell him not to strain to ignore their shouts; if he does, he's still paying attention to *them*. Instead, he should think only about the ball. Concentrate on it alone. Think only about how he's going to handle the ball. Visualize how it will feel in his hand right before he lets go. Picture how it will look when it flies past the batter or swishes through the hoop. He might even want to rehearse his "rabbit ears" defense in practice by having fellow teammates yell (in friendly jest), "You're gonna miss!!" right before he tries to make a key play.

The kid who can avoid rabbit ears in a game is the one his team will come to rely on in a pinch. And as he goes through life, he'll come to be known as one of those admirable people of strong character who know how to stand firmly in the face of public criticism and still do what's right.

96. How to Build a Sand Castle

What we become, we make of ourselves. From the same sand, one person builds a shanty, another a castle.

—A Good Dad Maxim

A sand castle looks easy to build—from a distance. But let a kid try it, and trouble erupts. After about twenty trips hauling tiny buckets of water to his construction site, the kid gets bored and the castle is forgotten.

But your kid's castle gets finished, complete with parapets, staircases, and flags snapping in the breeze. That's because you know the secret to building a sand castle: use lots of water— more water than lesser builders would ever imagine.

Though some sand is powdery and flat, most sand is round. Ever try piling ten thousand marbles four feet high? Well, that's what a kid's doing when she builds a sand castle. Water is the cement that holds those little marbles together.

So start with a hole—a water hole. On a high, dry mound of beach fairly close to the water's edge (but not so close a rogue wave can reach it), have your kid dig until she hits water. She's aiming for *depth*, not for *width*. She may have to dig eighteen inches or deeper. Next, have your kid stir up the sand and water in the hole with her feet (she can think of her feet as the cement mixer). Good castle-building sand is sloppy wet and about as thick and goopy as oatmeal.

Walls can be made with sand "bricks" (figure a).

(a)

A tower is built with sand "flapjacks," one piled on top of the other (figure b). Be sure to have her taper the tower, making it narrower as it gets higher.

Once she's created a structure, she can carve the wet sand into magical shapes with a popsicle stick or a small plastic knife. She can smoothly slice a tower to create a nice, sharp,

(b)

clean line. But she should carve from the *top* of the tower down. Otherwise, crumbling sand will ruin her handiwork on the lower levels. One of the most dazzling effects is a "staircase." Simply have her make a sand ramp, around a tower if she wants to, then carve out the stairs. She can also carve doors and windows.

If a tower falls, remind her that sand castles never last forever. That's part of their charm. Too often in this busy world, we're so directed toward final goals we forget to have fun as we work. We know there are forces bigger than ourselves, but we forget to be humble. So teach your child just to enjoy the delightful process of building and leave destiny to the tides.

97.

How to Get a Toad to Live in Your Yard

Little friends can be great friends.

— Aesop, the Good Dad of Moral Tales

The toad is considered the fattest, ugliest creature on earth. Teach your child to take care of one. If a kid can love that toad, he's getting to the heart of compassion.

All living creatures, you can tell your child, have the same basic needs: freedom, good food, water to drink, and a home. So here's the secret to getting a toad to live in your yard: build it a house.

As good luck would have it, toads have modest tastes. A toad will even live in a pile of rocks or under an old rotten board. But you and your kid want your little guest to live in style. So get a clay six-inch flowerpot and lay it on its side in a shady, moist spot in your yard—perhaps in a flower garden. Bury about one-third of the pot in rich, damp dirt. A toad "drinks" by sitting in water and absorbing moisture through his skin. So put a small, shallow saucer nearby and fill it nearly full, so the toad can get a drink. If the cozy pot house is near a night-light that attracts lots of tasty insects, so much the better.

Will a toad move in? That's for the toad to decide. Nature can only be cajoled to do our will, never forced. But there's a good chance he will. And once he does, he may stay in the same home year after year, living there until your kid goes to college.

With his bumpy brown skin, pale belly, and buggy eyes, a toad is certainly no looker. But by building a toad home and making sure his little guest feels welcome, your child will come to recognize his kinship with all living beings. Even a toad deserves world-class service.

98.

How to Change the Spark Plugs on the Car

Orderly actions lead to orderly thoughts.

—A Good Dad Saying

To most kids, the power that moves a car down the road is as strangely mysterious as the Force in *Star Wars*. They know turning the ignition key makes the motor start and the car move. But why? Everything that happens under the hood remains a dark unknown.

Fortunately, you know how to demystify the motor for your kid. Teach him to change the spark plugs. But it's important that he does it right. The secret: he needs to change the plugs one at a time, so he won't mix up the wires.

If he confuses the wires and puts them back on the wrong plugs, the motor will go *sheeer, pop-pop-pop* down the street, misfiring like crazy. Either that, or the car won't start at all. So here's how to teach him to change the spark plugs correctly.

1. First, he should make sure the ignition's turned off. There's a lot of electricity running through those plugs—about 20,000 to 40,000 volts! And that can deliver quite a zap.

2. Now have him remove each spark plug wire, one at a time, by grasping the wire boot (the part that fits over the plug) at the top and using a twisting-pulling motion. Then he should take a spark plug wrench, put it over the plug and unscrew counterclockwise. Once the plug's loose, he can just reach down with his fingers, unscrew it completely, and pull it out.

3. Now it's time to put in the new plug. But, first, he has to gap it. Have him look in the car owner's manual to find out how far apart the electrodes on the plug need to be gapped. Then have him take a wire gap gauge and "gap" the plug. To do this, he simply inserts the right-size metal wire on the gauge into the space between the electrodes at the bottom tip of the plug. Then he taps down gently on the little-metal-bar electrode so it just touches the top of the gapping tool. There should be a slight dragging feeling as he moves the wire between the electrodes. If it's too tight, he should press the blade of a small screwdriver into the gap to wedge the electrodes apart.

4. Have him check for cracks in the porcelain on the plug. If he finds a crack, he should discard the plug.

5. Now have him screw the new spark plug in place. He should make sure he screws it in straight, not cross-threaded. Once it's finger tight, he can use the socket wrench to snug it up. Then have him replace the wire on the plug with a little snap.

6. Have him repeat steps 1–5 until the job's done.

Changing the spark plugs on a car sounds difficult to someone who's never done it, but it's surprisingly simple. Your kid will feel greatly accomplished knowing he can now perform a skill even many adults can't do. By working to keep the wires straight, he'll also have learned to be orderly in his work. And it has been said that order is heaven's first law.

99.

How to Walk on Your Hands

Man first learned to stand erect maybe three million years ago. We're not so sure when he started walking on his hands. Maybe when the circus came to town.

—A Good Dad Observation

All kids want to show off to prove they're unique and special. But not knowing how to do it right, they often show off wrong by being loud, obnoxious, or rude. Teach your kid how to show off in a happy, positive, push-back-the-envelope sort of way. Teach him how to walk on his hands.

The ability to walk on one's hands builds great physical confidence. It also helps a child develop upper-body strength and a good sense of balance. But there's a secret: he has to position his hands correctly before he stands on them.

Most kids will try to walk on their hands with their fingers pointed straight ahead. But the second they lose balance, they fall. To accomplish this truly impressive dad feat, a kid needs to position his hands in a special way (figure a). He has to twist his elbows and turn his hands inward with his fingers splayed as wide apart as possible. His hands literally form two small balancing "platforms." If he starts falling over backwards, he can use his pinkie and ring fingers to catch and hold himself up. If he starts toppling the other way, he can stay upright by using his thumbs and index fingers.

To walk on his hands, of course, a kid needs enough strength to support his own weight with his arms. So hold your child up by his legs and have him lift his body with his arms to see if he can do it. If he can't, he may want to lift a few weights or learn to shinny up a tree (see chapter 17) to build upper-body strength. But if he can, terrific! He's ready.

So first have him position his hands correctly, fingers pointed inward and spread wide (figure b). Then have him stand on one foot and kick up until he hits that sweet spot where he's balanced. At this point, his back will be slightly arched, with his feet bent back over his head, as shown in figure a.

Once he's up, he can start walking. If he starts falling over backward, he can use his pinkies and ring fingers for balance and "walk" faster to catch himself. If his feet fall, he can simply kick up again. He won't get it perfect on the first try, of course. But with practice, he'll make it.

And when he does, he'll realize he's mastered a skill few people possess, which will make him feel special. He'll also become bolder. We often hear people say, "I've always done things that way," or "That's just the way I am." But where would humans be if we had no courage to attempt the novel, to reach out for new frontiers? The kid who learns to walk on his hands will very likely become an adult who's not afraid to try something new.

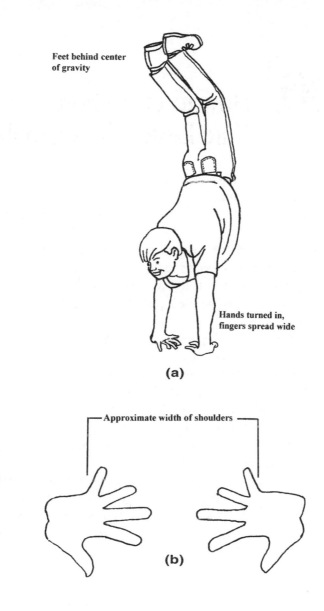

Feet behind center of gravity

Hands turned in, fingers spread wide

(a)

Approximate width of shoulders

(b)

235

100. How to Use Those Rare Letters in Scrabble

In Scrabble, don't curse your luck. Just make the best words you can with the letters you've drawn.

—A Good Dad Observation

A kid is at a big disadvantage when he plays Scrabble with adults. He just doesn't know as many good words. But you can teach him a few tricky words to even the score. And when he plays with kids his own age, he'll quickly become the unbeatable Scrabble champ.

Here's the secret: teach your kid a bunch of little words he can use to unload high-scoring letters.

When they draw those rare letters like *Z, Q, Y,* and *J,* most kids think they have to come up with a long, exotic word like *zedoary* or *sjambok.* So they hold onto their unusual letters for half the game, when they could be running up points. Break your kid of such wrong-headed "big is always better" thinking. Teach him little ways to score high.

Here are ten zingers, all just three or four letters, along with their definitions. If he manages to put any of these words on a triple-word box, he'll get a whopping forty-five to fifty-seven or more points.

azym: unleavened bread

fixy: fussy

mazy: confusing; like a maze

oyez: silence! a cry used by court criers to get people's attention before a proclamation.

pyx: a small box

quay: a small wharf

vizy: to look at closely

wiz: a wizard

zax: a roofing tool

zyme: enzyme; ferment

You might also want to provide him with a few "dumpers" (words to use when he's drawn too many vowels). A few juicy ones include: *aalii* (a small Hawaiian tree), *cooee* (an Australian bushman's warning cry), *guaiac* (a tonka bean), and *hoodoo* (a variation of voodoo), which means "bad luck"—to his opponent.

DAD TIP

How Your Kid Can Win a Scrabble Bet

So Uncle Fred has arrived for the holidays, and he fancies himself the Scrabble King of the Western World. Your kid offers a playful challenge: Is there any word in the English language that contains all five vowels in their correct order— *a, e, i, o, u*—plus the letter *y* (also used as a vowel)? In fact, there are two: facetiously and abstemiously. In case Fred asks, the latter comes from abstain and means being moderate in one's eating and drinking.

101. How to Photograph Lightning

Try, but don't strain; sometimes we just have to let the good things happen.

—A Good Dad Saying

To kids, lightning looks like some mysterious UFO. It appears out of nowhere, streaks across the sky, and disappears without a trace before anyone can observe it. Photographing such a phantom sounds impossible. Even if you had super-fast film in your camera, how would you know when to click? And what if the lightning struck you?

Fortunately, as a good dad, you know photographing lightning is a lot easier—and safer—than it sounds. To photograph lightning, here's the trick: you and your child have to do it at night.

Use regular film (ISO 100 or 200). Set up your camera in a dark, sheltered spot with a wide view of the sky. An attic window far away from streetlights will work great. Obviously, you want to take normal safety precautions and avoid setting up on a hill or underneath a tall tree.

Now aim your camera toward the most active area of the sky. Have your child hold the shutter open, or if you have a time exposure on your camera, just leave it open. She doesn't have to click at "just the right time." Because lightning blitzes across the sky so fast with such blazing light, it acts like a flashbulb and takes its *own* picture. After the fireworks, you simply close the shutter, then advance the film for the next brilliant appearance.

By learning to photograph lightning, your child will come to understand that nature is like a wise, loving mom. When you stop trying to run the show and just follow her lead, you can achieve amazing results. Always listen to your mother.